Latymer Upper School

A History of the School and its Foundation

Richard Villages and Thomas Easton, and their heirs
Churchman vicar of the said parrish, and the
for then churchwardens of the said parrish, and to other
named upon full trust hope and confidence as of this my last
will and testament in writing knowne for the better
and manifestation of my said trust hope and confidence
last before named onely, or the greater number of them
after my death, aboue nominate and shall eight poore
round of St Dunstons, being within the age of twelue
yeares a peece, and after such election by them made
onely, shall with the onely rent and proffitts of the said
said, rent and remainder for dublett of the said eight bond
of ffriese or leather lined with lynnen a shirte a paire
of shoos, and the said be ready made shall deliuer y
bond on the first day of Nouember Also that yearly
yett readie for euery of the said bond a dublett a
canuas lined with   a shirt a paire of wooll
and the said for ready made they, or some o.. my said
of the said bond on the last day of the Assension of o
that on the last floure, of euery of the said dublatts
shall troope of cloth, or baud be fasthnid and worne
the troope to be the Lattnent troope And also that
Latynent coate clums bond Also my desire is that
their coates or furnistens shall euery the said poore ba
to the end they maie learnt as well English, and their
attaine to the age of ffourteen yeares whereby to haue
vocons and also to instruct them in some work of thee
vertious want of euery of the said poore bond, or
of the said round of St Dunstons my said allowance of th
at unto for main of them as shall attaine to the said

Latymer Upper School

A History of the School and its Foundation

Nigel Watson

JAMES X JAMES

ISBN 0 907383 629
© Latymer Upper School 1995
First published October 1995

Printed and bound by BAS Printers Limited, Over Wallop, Hampshire

Designed by Bob Speel

New photography by John Spragg

Published by James & James (Publishers) Ltd
Gordon House Business Centre
6 Lissenden Gardens
London NW5 1LX

Picture Acknowledgements

*Many of the photographs were supplied by people closely connected with the School – Old
Latymerians, staff and parents. Thanks are due to: C O Grundy, W Böltger, J Shepherd,
S A F Davies, K J Coghill, G W Tait, F H F Mayo, J Gilbert, E N Foinette, G C Burger,
A Newman, A G Terry, P L N Brooks, A H Cox, R Williams, B G L Perkins, P Exel,
A R Watson, H J Millen, L V Chilton, D R Dover, R N Hobson and Spike Watson.*

*The pictures on pages 19, 23, 32, 37, 38 (top), 47, 76 (right), 77, 92, 103 (top left and right),
108(top), and 114 (photograph by Christine Bayliss) are copyright Hammersmith County
Library. Other pictures are copyright as follows: Sir Ralph Lacey (page 62) The Imperial War
Museum; and in the List of Distinguished Old Latymerians: Will Hammer: Marvel Comics;
Sir Harold Spencer Jones: Godfrey Argent Studio; Robert Jenkins: Royal Borough of Kensington
and Chelsea Libraries; C R C M Hammond: Banking, Insurance and Finance Union; Harold
Trevor Mote: Harrow Library Services; Ian Pashley Gibb: The British Library; Michael
Edward Nelson: Reuters; Lord Walker: The House of Commons Library; Professor Perham:
St John's College Library; Joshua Rozenberg: BBC; Hugh Jones: Mark Shearman. Pictures of
Alan Rickman and Hugh Grant were kindly provided by their agents.*

Half-title page: *A Latymer boy of 1878.*
Title page: *Part of Edward Latymer's will relating to the '8 poore boyes'*

FOREWORD

This book is the story of our School, established in 1624 but celebrating in 1995 its first 100 years as an 'Upper' School in the current building in King Street.

But any school is much more than its site and buildings, more even than its traditions. Essentially a school is its people – its pupils, staff, parents and Old Boys. This is especially true of Latymer Upper where the character of the School is based squarely on the individuality of those who have built it.

Nigel Watson, the author, has written an account that tells the story of the people who have made Latymer Upper School – its founder, benefactors, governors, teachers, pupils and headmasters. He expresses their commitment, energy and humour and makes the School come to life on the page.

Nigel has been helped in his research by many of those associated closely with the School, and the records and illustrations they have constructed are truly fascinating. We are most grateful to all who have helped with this project but, in particular, to Chris Hammond, Head of Middle School. Chris's long record of service to the School has allowed him to focus his unrivalled experience and dedicated support to the preparation of this book.

It is my sincere pleasure to thank Nigel, Chris, James & James Publishers and the many others whose contributions have made this excellent book possible.

COLIN DIGGORY
SUMMER 1995

Author's Acknowledgements

It would have been almost impossible to complete this history without the kind and unfailing assistance of Chris Hammond to whom I give my grateful thanks. There were three main sources for the history. The most important source was the Foundation minutes, which survive from the very beginning of the Foundation in 1627. I am grateful to Michael Sharman, the Clerk to the Governors, who arranged for several large tin boxes containing the minutes of the Foundation to be brought from the depths of the vaults of the local bank for the first time in years. Secondly, the successive volumes of the school magazine, *The Latymerian*, were invaluable and I thank the school librarian, Colin Appleton, for enabling me to look through them. Thirdly, I was able to conduct a limited number of interviews with past and present pupils and members of staff. I would therefore like to thank for their kind co-operation the following who were interviewed for this book: Matthew Bond, L V Chilton, Colin Diggory, Jack Edelman, Geoff Gurney, Maurice Isaac, Sir John Killick, Fred Mayo, Tony Parish, Martin Pavey, George Terry and Alan Watson. Nigel Orton and his band of helpers exchanged notes with me on Old Latymerians. Of the remaining sources, much reliance has been placed for the story of Edward Latymer upon Wheatley's thoroughly researched *The History of Edward Latymer and His Foundations*, while Davies's characterful account of *Latymer Upper School 1895–1967* was very helpful for the early years of the school. Any errors which remain can therefore safely be ascribed to me. Hamish MacGibbon and Bob Speel from James & James as usual gave me their helpful guidance throughout this project.

Nigel Watson
Spring 1995

CONTENTS

CHAPTER ONE

'Our Pious Founder'

EDWARD LATYMER

1556–1626

We commemorate before God the merits of
our pious founder, Edward Latymer, and the
labours of those who have built on his
Foundation. (The Latymer Prayer)

Charities have had a long and distinguished role in English education. The progress made by the state education system over the last century has made many of them redundant. Often the aims of those which have survived have become much broader than their original educational aims. Yet even today there are many charities throughout the country, both old-established and new, which continue to contribute towards the education of the nation, perpetuating a tradition which stretches back to the Middle Ages.

One of these is the Latymer Foundation, which administers the Latymer Upper School in Hammersmith, and can trace its origins back to the will of its pious founder who in 1624 directed that part of his wealth should support the clothing and education of "eight poore boyes" from Hammersmith.

The roots of the Latymer family can be traced as far back as 1463 to the village of Freston in Suffolk which lies some four miles from Ipswich on the south side of the River Orwell. The most distinguished member of the family was Edward Latymer's father, William. He was probably born at Freston about 1498. Educated at Corpus Christi College, Cambridge, he became a clergyman, as did many educated men of the time, and soon held several livings, a common practice at the time because of the shortage of clergymen and the poor income that many livings paid. In 1538 Latymer was appointed as Master of St Lawrence Pountney College in London, which had close links with his old Cambridge college, and he remained there until it was dissolved in 1547.

William Latymer does not seem to have been a very likeable man. Like the Vicar of Bray nearly 150 years later, he bent with the prevailing political wind. When his own bishop, Bishop Bonner of London, preached a sermon in 1549 which was less than expected by the supporters of the young king, Edward VI, Latymer was a principal witness against Bonner at his ensuing trial which

Opposite page: The Court of Wards and Liveries, late seventeenth century, where Edward Latymer was a Clerk to the Receiver-General. The Clerks in the picture, who are not named, are the three men at the foot of the table, facing the Master of the Court, Lord Burghley, who sits at the head of the table.

Freston Church in Suffolk. The roots of the Latymer family were in Freston.

resulted in him being thrown into prison. When Edward was succeeded by his sister, Mary, in 1553, the religious climate quickly changed. Latymer had been a prominent supporter of permitting priests to marry which had been enshrined in legislation in 1549. This was now repealed and married priests, including Latymer, were stripped of their livings. Faced with a choice between reviving his church career or renouncing his wife, Latymer took two years before deciding to choose the latter course, after which he was rewarded with a number of livings in quick succession. His career culminated in his appointment in 1560 as Dean of Peterborough and Prebendary of Westminster, and he held both offices until his death in 1583. At Peterborough he is reputed to have been instrumental in securing the restoration of the cathedral after years of neglect. His annual earnings from his salary as Dean and his stipend as Prebendary of £141 seem paltry today, but since the pound sterling in 1500 is reckoned to have been worth well over £300 in today's values, William Latymer was financially very comfortable. This was reflected in the long list of fine furnishings and house contents recorded in his will.

Many of those furnishings and contents were inherited by William Latymer's son, Edward. He was born about 1556, quite late in his father's life, and spent his childhood years in the Deanery at Peterborough. With his knowledge of the ups and downs of his father's clerical career, as the fashion for religion changed from one decade to the next, it was unsurprising that after matriculating as a pensioner of St John's College, Cambridge, in 1571, Edward should have chosen to enter the law rather than the Church. As William Harrison wrote in his *Description of England*, published in 1557 at a tempestuous time in the history of English religion, "the greatest part of the more excellent wits choose rather to employ their studies unto physic and the laws, utterly giving over the study of the Scriptures for fear lest they should in time not get their bread by the same".

Little is known about Edward Latymer's career between 1571 and 1594, although he was involved in the conveyance of rectorial tithes at Mildenhall in Suffolk in 1591. In 1594, however, he was appointed as a clerk in the Court of Wards. This had been established in 1540 to take over the administration of wardships from the Exchequer. Wardships occurred where the heir of a deceased tenant-in-chief who held land directly from the Crown was under-age at the time of the tenant's death. The Crown often retained the wardship but it became an increasingly common practice, fostered especially by Henry VII, to sell the wardship, along with the marriage of the ward, to the highest bidder. Wardships were attractive propositions. For the buyer they combined a sound investment in land and property with a good marriage match for one of his offspring. For the Crown as seller, they were a ready source of revenue for an Exchequer that was often hard-pressed for cash.

Among the officers of the Court of Wards was the Receiver-General who was in charge of receiving the revenue from the sale of wardships and of making any necessary payments. The Receiver employed two clerks and two auditors to assist him. When the then Receiver died in March 1594, there were several applicants for a post which as well as an attractive salary also brought many perks. After intensive lobbying William Fleetwood was appointed to the position at the end of May 1594.

Fleetwood wanted an able deputy and clerk. The vacancy was brought to Edward Latymer's attention by his friend, Richard Orrell, an Usher in Chancery, who knew about it from his friend, Henry Fleetwood, the Receiver-General's younger brother. Latymer drafted a letter advancing his cause for Orrell to copy in his own hand to Henry Fleetwood, intimating that the better the terms Fleetwood could arrange with his brother for Latymer, the more generous Latymer would be in his thanks. The result was that Latymer was appointed to the post at an annual salary of £30, whose meagreness was made up by the deputy's entitlement to certain additional fees.

Latymer remained in the post until 1601 and his duties appear to have mainly involved the keeping of accounts. The completion of the annual audit was evidently an event worth celebrating. In 1596 Latymer recorded that "uppen Friday ... I delivered to Mr Auditor from Mr Receiver £5 to buye him a hoggeshedd of wyne and the next morning to Mr Curle [the assistant auditor] £4, to Mr Lovelace [the auditor's clerk] 30s. and 10s. more I have for Mr Carter [the

Receipt, signed by Edward Latymer, of his father's stipend as Prebendary of Westminster.

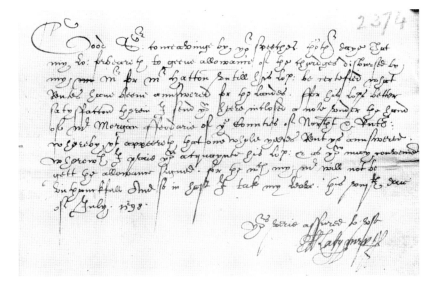

Letter written by Edward Latymer in 1598. At this time Latymer was deputy to the Receiver-General of the Court of Wards.

11

St Dunstan-in-the-West, where Edward Latymer worshipped, and where he was buried on his death in 1626.

junior audit clerk]". As a postscript he added "Memorandum, yt was geeven more liberally in respect yt was the first accompt".

After seven years as the deputy to the Receiver-General, Edward Latymer was appointed to fill a vacancy as one of the Court's two sworn attorneys. The work seems to have been repetitive and uneventful as far as the attorneys were concerned. During the plague which afflicted London in the summer of 1625, the Courts were adjourned and all business was suspended except that which attorneys could perform. Latymer continued to practise in this post almost until his death in early 1626.

Only generalisations can be made about Edward Latymer's character. He was obviously well-connected and knew many people of influence. His length of service as an attorney suggests that he was both competent and trusted. For many years he lived in Fleet Street and worshipped at the church of St Dunstan-in-the-West. His contribution of 22*s*. towards the repairs undertaken at the church in 1615 was one of the most generous individual donations made. In the same year he bought a house in the country at Edmonton with a barn, garden and orchard, and until his death he divided his time between his house off Fleet Street and his country home in Edmonton. As a man of some wealth Latymer lived well. His household effects included a clock, gilt and silver bowls, Canary cups and damask napkins, flaxen sheets and Turkey-work chairs. Among his personal belongings were his linen and ruffs, a small silk purse and a gold and diamond ring.

Latymer died in early January 1626 and as he had instructed he was buried in the south aisle of St Dunstan-in-the-West, where he had worshipped for many years. Latymer had wanted a sermon to be preached at his funeral and it seems likely that the vicar of the time would have done so. In 1626 the vicar of St Dunstan-in-the-West was the great poet and preacher, John Donne. Latymer's funeral pageant, a custom of the time, was impressive. His corpse was accompanied to the grave by 66 poor men clad in mourning who were given a shilling each to pay for their dinner on the day of the funeral.

Like many men of the period, Latymer's thoughts as he grew older had turned towards the prospects for his soul after his death and the perpetuation of his memory upon earth. With both these in mind he had purchased the manor of Butterwick in Fulham in 1622, paying £1,600 for the manor's 88 acres. This was to provide for the most substantial of the bequests he made in his will but there were many others besides. Some recalled his earlier life. In the parish of his birth, the city of Peterborough, and the parish in which he died, the poor benefited from bequests of £20 each. Other bequests were for the enhancement of the life on earth of his fellow men. He gave £200 to provide a better start in life for poor young men and women wishing to be married. Another £200 was bequeathed for the discharge of debtors from London's prisons. He cancelled many personal debts and left gifts worth more than £2,500 to his family, friends and servants. Twelve of his closest friends were given memorial rings inscribed with the words "*Mors mihi vita*" ("Death to me is life").

The will of a wealthy man created interest among distant relatives and two of them pursued Latymer's executors through the courts for several years as they appealed for the terms of the will to be set aside. There was never any real likelihood that they would be successful but the executors paid a small sum to settle the case out of court in 1633. Edward Latymer's last wishes could now be carried out without hindrance.

The Revd John Donne DD, vicar of St Dunstan-in-the-West at the time of Latymer's death.

Latymer's coat of arms, on the foundation stone from the Latymer Foundation School, preserved at Latymer Upper School.

13

The names of the Eyght
poore boyes and Syx wise men first
elected elected and Chosen by
the said offecers this ffirst
day of Iuly 1627

The poore eyght boyes

1. william Barrett the sune of Lambert Barrett
   borne 16 may 1620

2. Edorye Burton the sune of Edoryd Burton
   borne 2 of aprill 1620 as it is sayd

3. william Burton the sune of willm Burton Jun
   borne 8 october 1618

4. william Iordan the sune of Iohn Iordan
   borne 5 september 1619

5. Iohn ffinie the sune of Iohn ffinie of Iamarid 1617
   borne september 3,

6. Thomas Morsse the sune of Tho Morsse
   borne 14 ffeb: 1618

7. Iohn Leager the sune of widow Leager
   George borne 16 ffeb: 1616

8. Henrie Boyer the sune of Iohn Boyer september 25 1617
   borne 3 ffeb 1615

The Syx men

1. Iohn Naylor	Richard Cheese
2. Thomas Hughes	Edmond Powle
3. Iohn Eaton	Thomas Hill
Richard Vaughan	Tho. Hill
4. ffrancis Byrd	Io. Hart
5. Henrie Burton	Robert Ford
6.	Wm Ireland
	Tho: Manwayring

Iohn Holden Tho. Chase
william Burton Iohn Hill
Thomas Holden Iohn Man:
Churchwardens

Henry Marsh
Richard Maxwick
Tho. Morgen

CHAPTER TWO

'Keepe Them from Idle and Vagrant Courses'

The Latymer Foundation

1627–1878

Edward Latymer left nearly half the land he owned in Fulham in three parcels of varying sizes to the parochial trustees of St Dunstan-in-the-West, Edmonton and Fulham respectively. The profits from the parcel of less than six acres bequeathed to St Dunstan's were to be used to buy wheaten bread for the poor of the parish. Latymer's will stated that every Wednesday morning after prayers 12 of the parish's elderly poor were each to be given a pound loaf of bread. The procedure was to be repeated with 12 penny loaves of similar bread every Friday morning. This ceremony continued for more than 200 years but as the nature of the parish altered and its population declined there were fewer and fewer suitable candidates for Latymer's charity. In 1883 the charity was absorbed by the City Parochial Foundation.

Latymer left his country house in Edmonton to the local parish as well as eight-and-a-half acres of land in the parish of Fulham. The latter estate was located in Hammersmith which formed part of the parish of Fulham until it became a parish in its own right in 1834. The land lies north of Hammersmith Road, in the area of Brook Green, and its links with Edward Latymer are still perpetuated by the name of the large block of flats, Latymer Court, which was built on the site in the 1930s. Latymer's will instructed the Edmonton trustees to clothe and educate eight poor boys from the parish in terms identical to those applied to the parochial trustees of Fulham. The Latymer bequest was neither the first nor the last to be made for the education of Edmonton boys. In 1739 all these individual charities were amalgamated and a school house and buildings were acquired. As the value of the charity's property increased, it was able to educate more and more boys. By 1811, when new school premises were built, there were 75 boys on the school roll. Ninety years later, in 1901, a new scheme governing the charity was drawn up. This provided for the erection of a Lower or Elementary School which was built in 1903 and came under the control of the Edmonton Education Committee in 1904. The Upper School continued in increasingly unsuitable conditions in the old school buildings until a new school was built in Hazelbury Road in 1910 which admitted both boys and girls. The old school was demolished in the following year. Latymer

Opposite: The eight poor boys and six men who were the first beneficiaries of Latymer's will in 1627.

Sir Hugh Myddleton, nominated by Latymer to be one of the trustees of the Latymer School at Edmonton.

The Free Grammar School, Edmonton, 1750.

School, Edmonton, continues to thrive as a successful state secondary school.

On 21 June 1627 Latymer's executors conveyed to the Fulham trustees the 18 scattered parcels of land, totalling 28.5 acres, which Latymer had owned in the parish. It is this date which properly marks the beginning of the Latymer Foundation at Hammersmith. There were 20 original trustees of the Foundation and their names are dutifully recorded in the first minute book. From 1627 onwards the trustees and subsequently the board of governors have always included by right the vicar and churchwardens of Fulham and then St Paul's, Hammersmith.

Latymer's bequest to the Fulham trustees combined a concern both for the elderly poor and for the education of poor boys. As far as Hammersmith's aged poor were concerned, the trustees were directed to provide 10s. a year and a cassock or coat to "sixe poore aged men of good and honest conversacion". These six poor men were to be known as "Latymers Almesmen" and to distinguish them as such were to wear the Latymer cross in red material on the left sleeve of their coats.

The will also directed the trustees to "elect, nominate and chuse eight poore boies inhabitinge in the said towne of Hamersmith and beinge within the age of twelve yeares apeece and above the age of seaven yeares apeece". They would be called the "Latymers poore Almes boies" and would also wear the distinctive red Latymer cross on the left sleeve of their doublets. The profits from Latymer's property were to be used at Ascensiontide every year to provide them with "a doublett and a paire of breeches of course canvas lined" and "alsoe a shirt, a paire of stockins and a paire of shooes"; and on 1 November (All Saints' Day) every year to "provide and gett ready for everie of the said boies a doublett and a paire of breeches of frise cloth or leather, one shirt and a paire of stockins, and a paire of shooes". From 1628 onwards Ascension Day was celebrated each year by paying for refreshments for the boys (in 1628 1s. was spent upon "bread and beere") and this custom was extended to All Saints' Day in 1637. In addition to clothing the boys twice a year, Edward Latymer also stated that his trustees "shall cause the said eight poore boies to be putt to some petty schoole to thend they

The Latymer School, Church Street, Edmonton, 1811–1910.

may learne to read English and to be soe kept at Schoole untill they shall attaine to the age of thirteene yeares, thereby to keepe them from idle and vagrant courses and alsoe to instruct them in some part of God's true religion".

On 1 July 1627 the trustees met to elect the first eight poor boys. The latters' names deserve to be recorded in full:

> William Barrett, the son of Lambert Barrett, born 16 May 1620; George Burton, the son of George Burton, born 2 April 1620; William Burton, the son of William Burton junior, born 8 October 1618; William Jordane, the son of John Jordane, born 5 September 1619; John Finch, the son of John Finch, born 3 January 1617; Thomas Morse, the son of John Morse, born 24 February 1618; John Lather, the son of Widow Lather, born 16 February 1616; George Soper, the son of John Soper, born 25 September 1617.

Of these boys, six served out their time at school until the age of 13, William Burton was expelled for truancy, and John Finch died in 1628 at the age of 11.

Because there were no suitable facilities in Hammersmith the boys were sent to be taught in Fulham. It was a two-mile walk from Hammersmith along a country lane which passed through Fulham Fields. This was little more than a track and was often impassable in winter. The school at Fulham formed part of a building recently erected over the church porch which had the vestry chamber on its upper floor and the school-room on the lower floor. Its erection had been partly funded by a bequest from the estate of Dr Thomas Edwards, Fellow of All Souls, Oxford, and Chancellor to the Bishop of London, who died in 1618. Here the boys were taught until 1648 apart from a brief period between 1633 and 1636 when they returned to Hammersmith.

Every quarter the boys were examined by the trustees in reading and writing, which was all that the curriculum consisted of at this time. It seems to have been difficult to persuade the boys to improve their standard of learning since the trustees resolved from December 1631 onwards to threaten with expulsion those who did not perform satisfactorily. Boys who played truant or otherwise paid little attention to their education were subject to a similar threat and the trustees had no hesitation in censuring parents as well as boys for poor results or misbehaviour. In 1630, for example, Richard Evans and his mother were instructed to appear before the trustees to give a satisfactory explanation for his absence from school, failing which he was to be expelled. In the same year, Will Burton's truancy earned him the distinction of being the first boy to be expelled from the school, while Lawrence Smith, described in 1635 as a very unsatisfactory boy, was "put out for example's sake" only to be reinstated upon his promise to mend his ways.

The trustees realised that the boys could make real progress in their learning only if they were properly taught. This was rarely the case. Masters came and went with rapidity and in 1648, after the failure of yet another schoolmaster, the trustees decided to bring the boys back to Hammersmith. The opportunity to do so had arisen from the recent erection of a school in Hammersmith, as the minutes of the Foundation recorded on 30 April 1648:

> That in regard of Mr Ranton's neglect of the Teaching of the said Almesboyes and the opportunity of another scoole in the towne of

St Paul's Church, Hammersmith, and the eastern end of the first Latymer School, 1756–1863.

Hamersmith, that the said Lattimers boyes shall be forthwith removed from Mr Ranton and put to scoole to Mr Palmer and Mr Bull, masters of the schoole lately erected in the town of Hamersmith, and the summer of six pounds a year is to be allowed to the said Mr Palmer and Mr Bull for the care and education of the said Boyes in Religion and Learning.

Mr Palmer did not last long, however, asking to be relieved of his duties within the year. For the next eight years the boys were passed from one schoolmaster and schoolroom to another until in 1657 they were moved to the new parochial school house close by the church of St Paul's, Hammersmith, which had been consecrated as a chapel-of-ease in 1631. On this site Latymer boys were educated for more than 200 years.

During that period the trustees were able to fund the education of more and more boys as the income of the Foundation rose. As well as the increasing profits derived from the rising value of the Foundation's original endowments, the gifts of several more benefactors were added to the Foundation's capital. In 1679 one of the trustees, Ralph Gregge, left the Foundation £50 to invest in land, using the profits to educate one poor boy. The first boy to benefit from Gregge's legacy was William Oger in 1684. In the following year Isaac Le Gooch, a Dutch jeweller living at Hyde Lodge in Hammersmith, left his property to Ann Billingsley for the duration of her lifetime. He directed that upon her death, which occurred in 1692, half the profits from his land should be left to the Dutch Church in London (Austin Friars) and the other half, after the deduction of £10 a year for the reader of divine service at St Paul's, to the Latymer trustees. This funded the education of three more boys, the first being Richard Harris,

Hammersmith from the Thames, from a print of 1752.

William Gosling and William Swayne in 1694. From 1727 onwards the boys maintained by the Gregge and Le Gooch bequests wore as a distinguishing mark either the letter "G" or the letter "L" on their sleeves in addition to the Latymer cross. In the same year Colonel Nicholas Goodwin, another trustee, left the Foundation £20. The Margravine of Anspach, who lived at Brandenburgh House in Hammersmith, donated £10 to the Foundation in 1748. Finally, Peter Brushell, a treasurer of the Foundation, bequeathed £100 in 1767 for the maintenance and education of one poor boy.

Additional funds allowed the trustees to do two things. Firstly, they were able to educate more and more boys. Until the early eighteenth century the greater part of the Foundation's income was spent on providing the boys with two suits of clothing every year, an item relatively more expensive then than now. In 1656, for example, the total income of the Foundation was £30 18s. 11d. Out of that came the cost of the boys' winter suits as follows:

46 yards of woollen cloth	£9 4s. 6d.
26 ells (an ell measuring 45 inches) of lockram for shifts and linings for breeches	£1 6s. 6d.
Eight hats	£1 10s.
Eight pairs of shoes	15s. 6d.
Eight pairs of stockings	11s. 6d.
24 dozen buttons	5s.
A quantity of thread, hooks, eyes and points	3s. 2d.
Paid to the tailor for making up the coats and suits	£1 8s.

For the summer suits the trustees paid out as follows:

19

15 ells of Brown Holland cloth	£1 5s.
32 ells of lockram for shifts and linings	£1 12s.
Eight pairs of stockings	11s. 6d.
18 dozen buttons	1s. 2d.
Hooks, points and thread	2s.
To the tailor	16s.

Clothing the boys cost the Foundation a total of £20 7s. 4d. The remaining £9 9s. was accounted for by the schoolmaster's fees of £6, £3 paid to the six almsmen and 9s. paid as quitrent, a form of rent dating from medieval times, to the bishop. There was a surplus of £1 1s. 7d. It was not until the nineteenth century that the Foundation spent more on education than on clothing. In 1818, for example, clothing consumed 58 per cent of the Foundation's income. Even so this was a marked improvement upon the proportion spent upon clothing a hundred years earlier and the gradual growth in the Foundation's income allowed the trustees to spend more money on educating more boys. By 1715 therefore the Foundation was educating 20 boys. This was reduced between 1756 and 1779 to 15 boys but by 1783 the number of Latymer boys had risen to 30. During the nineteenth century there was a steady increase in numbers:

1817	50	1820	90	1851	100
1818	70	1844	90	1870	125

By the latter year the Foundation's income had grown to £604 a year.

Secondly, in order to accommodate more boys, it was necessary to improve and enlarge the school building at regular intervals. By 1755 the Hammersmith school building was in a ruinous condition. The trustees decided to demolish it and replace it with a larger building, although this still measured only 17 feet wide by 30 feet long. The new building was two storeys high with school rooms on both floors, a committee room for the trustees and a small room for the resident mistress. The provision of two school rooms and accommodation for the mistress was necessary because the Latymer boys and the girls educated by the Female Charity School had been taught under the same roof since 1726. The two charities had become closely linked at that time and were now administered by the same trustees. In addition there were at least 20 other children in the school under the auspices of various other charities. The new school with its two school rooms allowed boys and girls to be taught in the same building at the same time in separate rooms. Previously, in the old school building with its single room, they would have been taught at different times of the week since mixed classes were rarely permitted. But the cost of building the new school proved to be such a drain upon the Foundation's resources that the number of boys had to be reduced from 20 to 15 until 1779. Numbers were only restored when the debt incurred by the trustees had been paid off.

Further increases in the number of boys at the school during the nineteenth century necessitated further expansion of the school buildings. In 1818 the trustees' committee room was taken over as an additional classroom to provide space for an extra 30 boys. In the next year two more rooms were added to the west end of the building, with the necessary sanction from the Charity

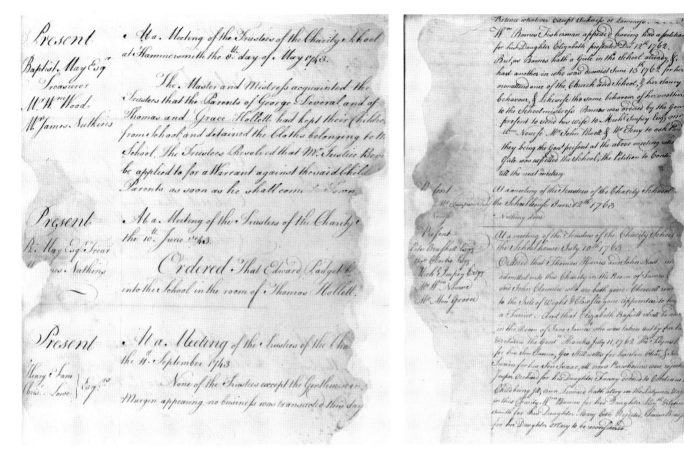

Commissioners, formed in 1818 to regulate the administration of the thousands of charities up and down the land.

There was no further change until the 1860s. By then there were only a handful of girls being educated by the Female Charity School. Unlike the Latymer Foundation, the Female Charity School had never been well-endowed and its income declined steadily over the years. With insufficient money to continue running the school, no further admissions were made after June 1861 and in 1863 the remaining girls were transferred to the adjacent St Paul's National School, opened in 1836, and the charity was wound up. By contrast, the Latymer Foundation was flourishing in terms of the numbers of boys now attending school. The problem was that there were 100 boys crammed into buildings intended to accommodate 60. The buildings were old-fashioned, there was no master's house, no playground, and the site was too small for any further expansion. The trustees agreed in August 1860 to request the permission of the Charity Commission to erect a new school for 125 pupils on land owned by the Foundation in Hammersmith Road at a cost not exceeding £1,500.

Now for the first time the trustees came up against the bureaucratic delays which were to plague their later plans for the Latymer Upper School. It was only in March 1861 that the Charity Commissioners visited Hammersmith to enquire into the Foundation, its endowments and objectives, in relation to the proposals for a new school. Two months later the Commission gave its approval of the new school but further negotiations over the plans of the school delayed a start upon the foundations until the beginning of September 1862. It was the way of things even then that actual building costs exceeded estimates and the final bill came to £2,140.

The new school was opened during a public ceremony on the morning of Thursday 24 September 1863. The procession, which took 15 minutes to wind its way from the site of the old school to the site of the new, was led by the Latymer boys and their masters. Behind them followed the almsmen, representatives of the builders and architects, visitors and clergy, with the trustees bringing up the rear. 120 guests were invited to take wine and biscuits in the new school, each boy was given 6d. and each almsman a shilling, and the trustees and their special guests dined in the schoolroom that evening.

Improvements to bricks and mortar were only one aspect of the trustees' educational responsibilities. The trustees continued to take an interest in the quality of the education offered to the boys and the level of achievement they attained. But their interest over the years appears to have been somewhat haphazard. There was a regular cycle of years of inattention to how the boys were taught punctuated by the occasional external inspection followed by stern reprimands to the schoolmasters to improve matters. This pattern was partly the result of the way the trustees were appointed. It was usual for several to be appointed at once when there were a number of long-standing vacancies. They usually served until they died, retired or resigned, often serving for many years and carrying out their responsibilities well into their old age regardless of whether or not they were fit to do so. Occasional vacancies were rarely filled and it was only when a dwindling band of trustees was left in charge of the Foundation that it was recognised that urgent action had to be taken to fill the many outstanding vacancies. Long-serving trustees tended to become complacent and allow affairs to run on as they always had. Newly appointed, vigorous and active trustees usually took a more positive attitude towards their responsibilities.

In June 1726, for example, the newly-appointed trustees examined the boys and girls in the school and found them to be "very backward in their learning". The schoolmaster and schoolmistress were both ordered to be "more diligent in their employ" and asked to promise not to teach any additional children if it was to the detriment of the education of the existing pupils. The trustees felt that it was "proper" to issue a "Paper of Directions" to master, mistress and parents. The teachers were instructed to ensure that their pupils were well-behaved, attended school and church regularly, and that those who could read were able to sing a psalm. Parents were ordered to see that their children attended school between the hours of 7 am and 12 noon and again between 2 pm and 5 pm from April to September, the only alteration during the winter months being that school began an hour later at 8 am. They were also exhorted to ensure that their children were "clean and neat" (parents were held accountable for the cost of their clothes during the year) and that they never missed church on Sundays, to correct them at home for "cursing, swearing, or any other Profanities" and set them a good example, and to make sure that they wore their uniform "particularly in Publick". This had some effect as the pupils were found to read and write "tolerably well" when the trustees examined them in August 1734, reminding the

schoolmaster and schoolmistress at the same time "to use their utmost Diligence in improving them". The limited curriculum remained based upon reading, writing and religious instruction at church on Sundays. Anything broader would have been a radical departure from the spirit of the times. As Asa Briggs has remarked, "Such efforts were concerned not with refashioning the way of life of the poor but with keeping them in their due place in society by instruction in the scriptures and the catechism". Yet, extraordinarily, such limited attempts to educate the poor still came under attack from those who believed that such a process would undermine the fabric of society.

The next purge at the school was carried out by another set of 14 newly appointed trustees in the autumn of 1795. The new regulations they issued set school hours at 8 am to 12 noon and 1 pm to 5 pm daily. Each school day would start and end with prayers. The school would be closed for two weeks' holiday at Christmas, one week at Easter and one week at Whitsuntide. Half-holidays were every Wednesday and Saturday and other holidays were granted for the celebration of the King's birthday, the Queen's birthday, and Guy Fawkes Night. Other holidays were at the discretion of the trustees. Once again the trustees insisted that pupils should be clean, tidy, punctual and polite. It was emphasised to parents that they must keep their children's clothes in good order and each

Hammersmith Mall in 1800. The trees are "Queen Catherine of Braganza's Elms". Queen Catherine of Braganza lived in Rivercourt House, on land now owned by Latymer Upper School.

child was provided with half a yard of material every year for running repairs. To ensure these rules were being kept the trustees visited the school each week. The rules were issued in printed form to those parents who could read. Those who could not were summoned to attend a meeting of the trustees where the rules were read out to them and they were asked to make their mark in the minute book as a sign of their agreement. This exercise was repeated again two years later.

At the same time as these rules were drawn up, the trustees advertised for a new schoolmaster to succeed Mr Bassett, who had been in the post since 1783. The advertisement asked for applications from properly qualified candidates of good character and membership of the Church of England who would be required to teach 30 boys reading, writing and accounts, and maintain cleanliness and discipline at a salary of £50 a year. Robert Jackson was appointed but lasted less than a year before being replaced by William Newell who remained in the post until his death in 1823.

Newell's long service did not mean that the trustees were necessarily happy with the way things were done at the school. Several more trustees were appointed in 1819 when the school was being extended for the last time, and they took the opportunity to draw up rules, regulations and a timetable which conformed to the pattern of the educational system advocated by the "National Society for promoting the education of the poor in the principles of the established church", founded in 1811. The rules insisted upon morning and afternoon prayers, a short break of ten minutes at 11 am and 4 pm, instruction for each boy in how to fold his clothes, and upon spelling to be set as homework each evening for every boy. The regulations laid down that each boy should submit his copying to the master for inspection after every two lines had been completed, that at least one sum should be done each day, that scripture should be read in the morning and *Aesop's Fables* and Goldsworthy's *History of England* in the afternoon. Once a month the boys had to clean their leather breeches. Every Saturday they had to clean out the schoolroom and clean their shoes for church attendance the following morning. On Sunday afternoons they were instructed to learn the Collects of the day for examination on Monday morning.

The timetable set out an almost unbroken diet of copying, ciphering (arithmetic), and reading, although by now it appears that school began no earlier than 9 am. The only alteration in the curriculum since 1627 had been the addition of arithmetic. The boys had always received religious instruction, as the founder had wished, even if only at church every Sunday. Now a place was also found for the catechism and psalmody on a Saturday morning.

The enforcement of this regime seems to have been rather lax. After a catalogue of ill-discipline following the appointment of Mr Millward to succeed Mr Newell in 1823, which involved throwing stones, truancy, "obscene and profane language", and "incorrigible misbehaviour", for which seven boys were whipped and deprived of their Ascension Day dinner, the trustees insisted upon strict adherence to the rules and regulations. Deviation from them, the trustees believed, including the absence for some years of any morning or evening prayers, had been responsible for "the present disorderly and refractory Character of the School".

Millward nevertheless remained in his position until his death in 1841. This was despite the fact that the first external inspection of the school at the trustees' request in 1828 found "a want of energy in every department". Millward was assisted only by two monitors, that is, older children who were responsible for teaching the younger boys. In the days when money was short, teacher training was minimal, and teachers themselves were scarce, this was a cheap method for spreading the rudiments of knowledge. The advantages of the system were that it promoted responsibility, instilled discipline, and encouraged pupils to help each other. Its survival depended upon the prevalent trend of the time which regarded education as no more than "a mechanical process of instilling facts into the minds of children". The inspector at the Latymer school in 1828 found that such a system did little for the pupils. He found that the teachers had only a superficial knowledge of how to teach and therefore the whole school was in "confusion". Millward and his pupil assistants were despatched to the Central School in London to be trained in the Madras System of Education. Neither Millward nor the school appears to have benefited much. In 1835, when he was heavily in debt, had been arrested on the demand of one of his creditors, and was on the verge of bankruptcy, he pleaded with the trustees not to sack him. The trustees were merciful, Millward retained his job and avoided bankruptcy. But the trustees made clear that he was only on probation and his employment would be brought to an end "unless a great amendment is observed in the education and discipline of the Boys".

The second inspection of the school was requested by the trustees in 1840 so that they might have sufficient information on which to judge whether Mr Millward's application for a rise in salary was justified. The Reverend Dr Mitchell's report was critical. There was little attempt to train the children, there was no time-table or course of study in use, the children knew little history and were rarely questioned on the limited range of reading they were given (Aesop was still the only author read in school). He recommended the introduction of a weekly course of study, the purchase of more books of a general nature, and the decoration of the classroom with maps ("These things all help to civilise"). There is no record of whether Mr Millward received an increase in his salary.

By the time of Richard Hester's appointment as schoolmaster in August 1849, slates had finally given way to exercise books and the badges which had long been awarded for merit in spelling and handwriting were joined by merit badges in mathematics. The start of Hester's tenure coincided with yet another mass appointment of new trustees, this time numbering 12. It was not surprising that the new trustees requested a third external inspection of the school in the spring of 1850. The verdict on this occasion was less severe. While there was a need for more teaching staff, and a broader and more advanced curriculum, the inspector found that "The discipline is good and the Master appears to exercise his influence and authority without effort".

One result of the inspection was the decision by the trustees to form an educational committee which reported to the main body of trustees on educational matters. It persuaded the trustees to accept in principle the urgent need for an assistant master with a teacher training certificate, but this appointment was

Buttons worn by a Latymer Foundation boy. The number 94 refers to the accession number of the boy in the school register.

A Latymer boy of 1878.

delayed for various reasons until 1856. When the post became vacant again in 1861, it was filled by T W Pledger, who eventually succeeded Hester when he retired in 1872, and remained as head of the school through all its subsequent transformations until he too retired in 1907. He then became clerk to the Foundation for several years.

The educational committee also recommended to the trustees in 1853 that the school should be placed under the auspices of the Committee of the Council of Education and the state school inspectors. This government committee had not been in existence for many years but had already introduced the pupil-teacher system to replace the ineffective monitorial system. Pupil-teachers were apprenticed for five years to schools recommended by government inspectors and were eligible for grants to a training college, from which certificated teachers received an annual government grant in addition to their ordinary salaries.

By the 1850s parliament was granting more than £500,000 a year for education, a considerable increase upon the £20,000 first voted in 1833, but this was entirely for the purposes of state aid and supervision. Opinion was still not prepared to countenance a state education service. As far as the Latymer Foundation was concerned, the advantages of government assistance were the provision of two pupil-teachers paid for by the government. On the other hand, if the trustees refused further state inspections, they would become responsible for paying the pupil-teachers' salaries. The possibility of further parliamentary legislation on education caused the trustees to postpone any decision on the matter. The matter was raised once more in 1858 but the trustees decided not to apply for state assistance.

The school rules were re-written again in 1864 along familiar lines. The school day was to run from 8.45 am until 1.45 pm from Monday to Friday. Saturday was a holiday but the boys were expected to attend school at 10.00 am and 5.45 pm on Sunday before processing to their respective churches. They were also expected to attend the Sunday school run by the vicar during the afternoon. Boys were reminded that they should appear at all times "clean and tidy" and that their clothes and shoes were to be "thoroughly and neatly mended". They were forbidden to appear at school in anything other than "the regular dress of the Charity". By now this "regular dress" consisted of a blue flat-topped cap, blue swallow-tail coat with large brass buttons, waistcoat, shirt with a high collar, white linen bands worn around the neck, corduroy breeches, grey worsted stockings, and either boots or shoes. On the right arm of the coat the embroidered badge representing the Latymer cross was still worn. Since at least 1800 each boy had also worn on the left breast of his coat a large metal badge carrying a number corresponding to his number in the admissions register. The importance of the Latymer uniform was emphasised in another rule which insisted that boys must not be allowed "to play or loiter about the Church Yard, the Streets, the Shore of the River, or among the Barges; nor to use ill language, be rude, throw stones; or do anything to damage [their] Clothes".

By 1878, the year in which fundamental changes were made to the operation of the Latymer Foundation for the first time in its history, as we shall see later, it was reckoned that almost 2,400 boys had been educated under the auspices of the Foundation. As Edward Latymer would have wished, most of these boys were from poor Hammersmith families. The trustees also admitted poor children from the local workhouse. In the 1720s the workhouse children did not attend school every day, however, but came to school one day and laboured in the workhouse the next. By the 1740s the trustees had arranged for such children to attend school full-time but they frequently played truant. By the early 1800s the arrangement seems to have ended as one or two boys left the school before their time had expired with the comment "went into the workhouse" beside their names. One boy, George Samson, had to leave the school in February 1849 because of the death of his mother and presumably was also taken into the workhouse. It seems harsh to us today to deal in such a way with a nine-year-old orphan boy but that was the way things were. Similarly George Newman's education came to a halt in 1857 when he was transferred to the Soldiers' Orphan Asylum in Barnet after the death of his father on military service in the Crimea.

The register of applicants for admission maintained by the Foundation from 1850 onwards reveals the occupation of parents and illustrates how the trustees

Attendance card, 1872. Note the proverbs in the borders intended to improve the boys' conduct. The reverse side includes "It is better to be unborn than untaught".

adhered to the selection of boys who came from poor families. Included among the occupations of those families listed in 1850 were the following:

Gardener	Tailor	Ostler
Carpenter	Wheelwright	Cabman
Labourer	Turncock	Shoemaker
Maltman	Whipmaker	Laundress
Bargeman	Greengrocer	Charwoman
Coachman	Baker	Housekeeper

Although many of the occupations remained the same 25 years later, the inclusion of railway inspectors, tin-plate makers, engine-drivers, gas fitters, postmen and policemen marked the progress of the Victorian age.

The register provided the trustees with information on which to base their selection of boys for vacancies. In fact, the Foundation had already become more selective in its choice of scholars by the 1830s. In November 1835 one of the trustees, George Bird, proposed that children should be eligible for admission if they had not already been taught their "letters" and "first lessons" but his proposal was defeated by five votes to two. George Bird was one of several members of the Bird family, a well-known Hammersmith family of lawyers, who played a prominent role as trustees, treasurers and solicitors to the Foundation from the late eighteenth century until the early years of the twentieth. This involvement gave rise to unfounded allegations of undue influence and corruption made against James Bird, the Foundation's solicitor, in 1851 when such suspicions were put about the town on "public printed placards". James successfully sued his accusers for libel and sent the damages of £10 to the Foundation.

From 1850 onwards the Foundation register noted the name, address and occupation of the parents, the size of the family, the applicant's date of birth, his reading ability, the name of any previous school, and the parish of the parents. From 1856 it included whether or not the applicant had been baptised, from 1860 whether or not he had been vaccinated (vaccination had been required of all applicants since 1840), and from 1865 how long the family had been resident in the parish.

With an increasing number of places available from the early eighteenth century onwards, and a corresponding increase in applications to the trustees, there was pressure from applicants living outside the parish for admission. The trustees resisted such pressure and reaffirmed their adherence to the founder's wishes in 1735, 1745 and 1769. Exceptions were nevertheless made. In 1812, for example, 10-year-old James Crew "was admitted into the School through the respectability and good character of his Parents although not a Parishioner". The trustees also unanimously agreed in 1837 to permit existing pupils whose parents had moved out of the parish to continue at the school.

Boys entered the school at any age between seven and 12 and most left immediately after their thirteenth birthdays. During the late eighteenth century some boys appear to have been allowed to stay on at the school after the age of 13 since the trustees made a point in 1787 of reiterating Latymer's original instruction on the school-leaving age. For a variety of reasons boys often left before their time had expired. Sometimes parents took their boys away without explanation. Charles J Smith, later the first headmaster of the Latymer Upper School, entered the school in September 1865 but was removed without reason by his parents in October 1866. Occasionally boys ran away. In 1710 Isaac Paget ran away to sea at the age of eight after little more than a year in school, as did George Douglas in 1799 at the age of 12. Boys left the school because of illness, like William Jones in 1801, who was "Removed, being afflicted with the Evil", or John Clack in 1834 "on account of an infectious eruption on the skin". Several boys, like one of the original eight poor boys, John Finch, in 1628, never lived to see their thirteenth birthdays. From time to time the trustees gave their consent to the premature departure of boys who had already found employment. The trustees were always concerned to secure the future of their school-leavers if at all possible. In 1734 the trustees remarked that

> it is notorious that many of the Boys Educated in the Charity School when the time of their continuance therein Expires, either thro' the Neglect or the Necessity of their Parents, [are] left entirely to themselves, and live for the most part in a state of Soleness; by which means they Contract ill Habits, become a reproach to the Charity, and are absolutely useless to Society.

In order to prevent "such growing Evils for the future", the trustees insisted that the sons of tradesmen should be bound by their fathers to a subsequent trade apprenticeship before they were admitted to the school. For the sons of "any poor person" without any trade or profession, the trustees at their discretion ensured that they were apprenticed at the Foundation's expense to "any Farmer, Waterman, Bargeman, Gardiner or any other employment they shall approve". This system survived into the nineteenth century. In 1800, for example, the Foundation paid £3 to the father of one boy to enable him to be apprenticed to a sailmaker.

Expulsion was another reason for the early departure of boys from the school. Will Burton, one of the original eight poor boys, was the first in 1630 and he was followed by a stream of others over the years, like George Herring, expelled in 1845 for knocking on doors and ringing doorbells after a long series of misdemeanours, and Daniel Gillard, expelled in 1863 after he had been convicted of robbery and sentenced to 14 days' hard labour. He was not the first criminal member of the school. In 1834 Thomas Barnard was convicted of stealing slate pencils. Described as "a bad character", he was flogged and expelled. A convict-

Right: *Brandenburgh House, home of Queen Caroline. The house was built in 1625 by Sir Nicholas Crispe (below). Crispe gave money to the Latymer Foundation, and much later, in 1863, the Latymer Foundation swapped land with Crispe's charity, and used the land so obtained as the site of the Hammersmith Road school.*

accomplice was also flogged but escaped expulsion. Five years later 12-year-old Thomas Floyd was found guilty of stealing a watch, seal and chain. He too escaped expulsion but suffered considerable humiliation. He was publicly and severely flogged, kept in school at dinnertime for a week, when he was fed only bread and water, and had to wear his coat inside out as a mark of disgrace.

Discipline, as suggested above, was maintained in a straight-forward manner. In 1827 William Bryce, who had been guilty of swearing on several occasions, was kept locked up on his own until 8.00 pm every evening for a week. In 1835 Robert Middleton was "well flogged" for gambling in the street. The next year the trustees resolved to maintain a punishments register, to administer all school floggings by birch rod, and to use the leather strap instead of the cane for "slight offences". But discipline was not based entirely upon the rule of the rod. Boys were often suspended rather than flogged, apparently rather indiscriminately by the middle of the nineteenth century, when the trustees asked for every offence to be carefully investigated to justify such action since boys suspended from school often used to get into more trouble "by their being allowed to run the streets". On occasion there would be parental complaints about the punishment handed out to certain boys but they always met with very short shrift from the trustees. On the other hand it was common for the parents of boys who were leaving the school to attend a meeting of the trustees and express their gratitude for the education their sons had received.

It was not only the miscreants whose behaviour was recorded in the minutes of the Foundation. Mention has been made earlier of the recipients of the merit badges awarded each year. From 1853 onwards punctual attenders were rewarded with "a treat" and taken "to some public place of Instruction and Amusement". In fact the first such "treat" had involved all the schoolchildren two years previously when they had been taken on a day out to visit the the Great Exhibition of Industry of all Nations at the Crystal Palace.

Even in the early 1870s Hammersmith retained the atmosphere of a small

The funeral procession for Queen Caroline, led by the Latymer boys, and by the girls of the Female Charity School.

thronged by farmers, dairymen and corn chandlers. Queues of vehicles still formed outside the distillery in Fulham Palace Road waiting to take away grains and wash for the cows and pigs to be found in the Latimer Road and Acton areas. In this small community the boys of the Latymer Foundation formed a distinctive part. As one former pupil who entered the school in 1878 later recalled, "We boys in those days were always requisitioned to take part in any movement on behalf of the parish: we were always looked up to and our reputation was second to none". When George IV's notorious wife, Queen Caroline, died in 1821 while resident at Brandenburgh House in Hammersmith, the Latymer boys and the girls of the Female Charity School formed the head of the funeral procession as it moved through the town. They strewed the road as they went with flowers gathered the previous day from the gardens of leading Hammersmith residents. In February 1840, on the occasion of the marriage of Queen Victoria to Prince Albert, the boys and girls of the school lined up along the Broadway as the Queen passed by and were each treated to a large bun afterwards. Some years later the boys all attended the laying of the foundation stone of the west wing of the West London Hospital and in June 1880 were again on display as the Prince and Princess of Wales passed by on their way to celebrate the ending of tolls on the old Hammersmith Bridge. More regularly the boys took part every year in beating the bounds of the parish on Ascension Day. But all these traditions built up over more than 250 years were soon to be changed for ever.

31

The Latymer Foundation School.

CHAPTER THREE

'Enlarging the Usefulness of the Charity'

THE NEW SCHEME

1878–1895

By the time that the new Latymer school was opened in 1863, there was a growing recognition that English education was backward in comparison with many Continental countries. This feeling was confirmed during the 1860s as the wars of the period seemed to suggest that the more educated nations produced better soldiers than the less educated ones. The passage of the 1867 Reform Bill made the education of the masses an urgent problem. The growing acceptance by public opinion that the state should take a more direct role in education strengthened the hand of the Liberal government of 1868 in its desire to bring about reform.

The 1870 Education Act promoted by W A Forster was the start of the process of reform. It was a compromise measure, as it had to be given the sharp division of opinion between the secularists and the religionists which had been the biggest hindrance to reform throughout the century. It applied only to children under 13 and aimed to secure a sufficient number of schools throughout the country which were open to state inspection and maintained complete religious liberty. Locally elected school boards were established with the power to levy rates to fund the building of schools and the employment of teachers. The Act did not provide free education for all, only for the poorest parents who could not afford to pay school fees. It was nevertheless a momentous step forward as "henceforward there were no areas in England without schools and no children grew up without elementary education purely because their parents were poor".

Because the Act provided an elementary education for all children for the first time, there was little scope in the early years of the new system for the development of a liberal or even vocational curriculum. Elementary schools provided the sort of basic curriculum which the Latymer school had offered for many years. The pressing need was to conquer mass illiteracy. A measure of the success achieved by the new system came in the general election of 1886 when out of more than 2.4 million votes cast in England and Wales only 38,547 were those of illiterates. Attendance at school was made compulsory in 1880 and elementary school fees were abolished in 1891.

Until the elementary schools had become well-established there could be no secondary education for the poor. During the nineteenth century this was largely restricted to the middle and upper classes and remained almost entirely unreformed. The Taunton Commission of 1864 had discovered a great national need for secondary schools. At that time 100 towns with a population of more than 5,000 people were without a grammar school of any sort. Even where grammar schools existed, their curriculum often remained narrowly classical and few had taken the opportunity to widen the curriculum which legislation had permitted as long ago as 1840. There had been a renaissance among the public schools but these catered for a class above those who attended the grammar schools. The Commission did not advocate an end to this class-based system but did propose increased state assistance for secondary education.

Partly because the grammar schools remained unchanged, there were attempts made within the elementary system, where the school leaving age was 14, to provide an advanced education for the less well-off. Under the department of education, many school boards established higher grade elementary schools, with their own laboratories, apparatus, and art provision, which taught the syllabus of the Science and Art Department, whose exams brought grant aid to the participating schools. At the same time, during the 1880s and 1890s, when there was a concerted campaign to raise the standards of the nation's technical education, technical education boards with the power to levy on the rates were created under the charge of the Science and Art Department with the aim of providing an education of a secondary nature. Both these initiatives, under the control of different government bodies, failed to recognise existing grammar schools. It was evident that the "uncoordinated attempt to develop secondary instruction under an elementary school code, for children all of whom must leave at 14, could not be satisfactory". The recommendations of the Bryce Commission in 1895, which considered this situation, were therefore a major step forward, advocating the establishment of a central department of education (the Board of Education was created in 1899) and of local education authorities based upon existing counties or county boroughs (enshrined in the 1902 Education Act). In fact it was not until the 1902 Act that anything like the system of secondary education which continues today was developed.

Part of the foundations for that system had already been laid, however, with the work of the Taunton Commission. One of its recommendations had been to redeploy ancient endowments to create a hierarchy of schools corresponding to the various classes of society. Arising from the Commission's recommendations came the creation of the Endowed Schools Commission which had the power to revise the statutes of endowed schools. The Commissioners would have the power to appropriate parish charities for education and exercise control over any educational schemes subsequently devised. The Commission's work came in for a great deal of criticism and it was lambasted as "a small party of specious reformers, given to much talk and bent on giving laws to somebody". It was abolished in 1874 only for its powers to be absorbed by the Charity Commission who exercised them in almost exactly the same manner.

The trustees of the Latymer Foundation were aware of these trends during the late nineteenth century. They had had several dealings with the Charity

Commission in the past as, unlike many parochial charities, they were still actively involved in running a school. Before there was any evidence of the Latymer Foundation being requested to draw up a new scheme, the trustees were already giving consideration to the idea. In May 1872 they established a subcommittee to prepare "a scheme for enlarging the usefulness of the Charity". By the end of the year the trustees had won the support of the new London School Board for a proposal to erect a new elementary school at Hammersmith under the regulations of the 1870 Act. There was a brief discussion with the Charity Commission about the issue but the latter would say nothing other than that "the Endowed Schools Commissioners are likely to propose a scheme before long". Nevertheless the trustees, whose income now exceeded expenditure by £200 a year, pressed on with their own scheme. At the beginning of 1873 they forwarded a list of the changes they wished to make to the Charity Commission. They wanted to decrease the number of boys to 120. They wanted to limit their responsibility for clothing the boys to those in the first two classes of the school and raise the school leaving age to 14 to conform with that of the Act. To assist school leavers they wished to establish six leaving exhibitions of £10 a year. Finally they had abandoned any idea of establishing new elementary schools in Hammersmith and instead wanted to erect a Latymer secondary school for 160–200 boys, each making a weekly payment towards school expenses, and establish other similar schools in Hammersmith as funds permitted.

In fact, with the Charity Commission assuming the role of the Endowed Schools Commission in 1874, the trustees' proposals formed the basis for negotiations between the two sides. One of the sticking points between the two parties was the trustees' insistence that the elementary school in any new scheme should continue to be free. Since elementary school fees were not abolished until 1891, this was not something that the Commissioners could countenance. By the time a draft scheme was published in the summer of 1876, the Commissioners had agreed to compromise over the proposed elementary school. They increased the annual sum payable by the Foundation for the maintenance of the school but emphasised that it could not be totally free. The trustees accepted with reluctance. The sum agreed upon, £250, remained a bone of contention between the trustees and the education authorities for many years afterwards. The Charity Commission Scheme for the administration of the Latymer Charity, to give it its full name, was finally approved on 14 September 1878.

Latymer Foundation School

Plan of the Foundation School site, 1875.

The new scheme provided that the governing body of the Foundation should consist of 12 persons, including three ex-officio representatives of the parish church, three to be nominated by Hammersmith Borough Council, two to be nominated by the London School Board (the nominations were later transferred to the London County Council) and four co-optative members. Secondly, it set aside £75 a year to be spent upon six poor deserving aged men of good character residing in Hammersmith. Thirdly, the existing school, to be known in future as the Latymer Lower School (although it was more popularly called the Latymer Foundation School), was to be operated from 1 January 1879 as a public elementary school for boys at a maximum fee of 9*d.* a week although existing pupils would continue to attend free of charge. Religious instruction was to be in accordance with the Christian faith but religious exemption could be claimed.

These changes greatly altered the character of the Latymer Foundation School. There were only 35 Latymer boys on the school roll when the changes came into effect in January 1879. The last of them, Albert Tomes, left the school most aptly on 1 November 1881, bringing to an end a tradition more than 250 years old. The other 90 boys on the roll when the new school started paid a weekly fee of 4*d.* while those admitted thereafter were charged 6*d.* a week. Not one of the boys on the roll that January morning were dressed in the traditional Latymer uniform. That too disappeared and the boys now wore ordinary clothing.

The school quickly grew in strength. By 1882, when the Latymer Foundation School became classified as a higher grade school, there were 200 boys in attendance. It was overcrowded and there was an urgent need to provide more accommodation. Despite the fact that the school inspectors had recommended extending the school, the Charity Commission, bearing in mind the likely costs upon the Foundation of the other aspects of the scheme, gave in only reluctantly to sustained pressure from the board of governors. Additional buildings were approved in 1883 and in 1889 the Commissioners sanctioned an increase in numbers at the school to a maximum of 400. By the early 1890s the school, under the headship of T W Pledger, was well established. The curriculum now included not only elementary subjects but French, music, geography, algebra and basic science. Shorthand and bookkeeping were added soon afterwards. The school inspectors reported in 1892 that "Order, tone and instruction are all highly creditable to the staff". In the following year the inspector noted that "This school fully maintains its very good state of efficiency. All members of the staff work with zeal and industry and the instruction generally is skilful and thorough". The school was so popular that it already exceeded its notional maximum with 441 pupils in attendance.

The main emphasis of the 1878 scheme was upon secondary education. One aspect of this was that when all other parts of the scheme had been carried through then the Foundation should strive to establish a day school for girls along the lines of that proposed by the scheme for boys. But the most significant part of the scheme was the provision for a day school, to be known as the Latymer Upper School, for 150 boys. Entry was permitted to boys aged between eight and 16. Beyond the age of 16 boys would require the express permission of the governors if they wished to continue at the school. Admission by entrance examination would be open to "all boys of good character and sufficient health,

Athletics outside the Latymer Foundation School.

who are residing with their parents, guardians and near relations". Tuition fees would be set at a maximum of £5 a year although Foundation Scholarships would be created for the remission of fees for up to 10% of pupils. Half of the scholarships were to be awarded to applicants from either the Latymer Foundation School or other elementary schools in Hammersmith. In addition elementary school scholarships would be made available worth £10 a year for a maximum of three years. The scheme prescribed a curriculum the most striking feature of which was the inclusion of natural science with particular provision for experimental chemistry and practical mechanics.

The governors at once began to search for a suitable site for the new school. It was not until the spring of 1885, however, after lengthy and unexplained delays, that the minutes refer to a site for the first time. Sketch plans were produced for the Upper School "adapted to the site of Hyde Lodge", which had been the home in the past of one of the Foundation's benefactors, Isaac Le Gooch, as a result of which the Foundation already owned half. At the same time, however, the governors had also been approached by the trustees of the Godolphin School for Boys in Iffley Road. The school was in decline and under further pressure because of the removal of St Paul's School in 1884 from its location beside St Paul's Cathedral to its new site in Talgarth Road in Hammersmith. The trustees were prepared to consider any reasonable offer from the governors of the Latymer Foundation. Indeed, in December 1885, the governors resolved to buy the Godolphin School site although at the same time negotiations were continuing for the site at Hyde Lodge.

The two sites were carefully compared. Although the Hyde Lodge site was long and narrow, with a frontage of 80 feet and a depth of 900 feet, it was described as a very good situation. The Godolphin site was central and convenient and provided more accommodation than was then necessary for the proposed

DO NOT RUN.

Boys from the Foundation School at a swimming lesson at Lime Grove.

John Radcliffe, who lived at Hyde Lodge 1710-14. He wanted to build a hospital on the site, but in the end it was built at Oxford.

Upper School. The valuer remarked of the Godolphin site that "it appears desirable to purchase the property, especially as it is feared that two schools in the same locality might clash". Ultimately the governors had to reject the idea of the Godolphin site. The Foundation could not afford to buy the site, pay for the necessary repairs and conversion works, and still have sufficient funds available to maintain the proposed new school.

Negotiations for the acquisition of the Hyde Lodge site dragged on from June 1886 until December 1887 before the Dutch Church accepted £1,700 from the Foundation for its share of the property. The purchase was paid for from funds raised by the sale of Foundation property elsewhere to the London and North Western Railway Company. Plans for the new school were prepared by George Saunders, a local architect, for the governors by early 1888. Only in March 1889 did the governors discuss the plans with the Charity Commissioners. The latter were not helpful and there was a distinct impression from the meeting of a last-minute reluctance by the Commissioners to approve the governors' plans. Concern was expressed only now that the new school might harm other boys' schools in the area, notably the Godolphin School, and the Commissioners even dared to suggest that the Foundation bring forward a scheme for a girls' school in preference to the proposed Upper School. The governors were having none of it, pointing not only to proposals for other girls' schools in the area, but also to the need for strong links to be established between the Upper and Lower schools, as the intention was for the latter to provide half the Upper School's initial intake of 200 pupils. At the end of May 1889 the Commission at last gave their approval to the governors' plans to establish the Upper School.

That, however, was not the end of the struggle to see the scheme implemented. Now came problems over the plans themselves. The governors asked for the Commission's approval of the plans towards the end of 1889, asking at the same time for consideration to be given to increasing the size of the school from 150 to 300 boys. The most pertinent point made by the Commission was about the

Hyde Lodge, half-owned by the Latymer Foundation since 1685, which bought the balance in 1886 as part of the site for the new school.

unsuitability of the site. In June 1890 the Commission wrote to the governors that "the efficiency of the buildings ... is affected by the conformation of the site – the unsuitability of which is indeed commented on by the architect as well as the risks in respect of light which from the extreme narrowness it is necessarily attended". The governors were asked to reconsider the suitability of the site, even to the extent of searching for a more appropriate site elsewhere in the parish. That was the last thing that the governors wanted to do after putting in so much time and effort to the planning of the current site. What they did do, however, was ask the agents for the adjacent property, Upper Mall House, whether the owners would be prepared to sell. The negotiations were somewhat protracted and it was not until April 1891 that a price was agreed for Upper Mall House of £3,000. This purchase almost doubled the size of the site and entirely satisfied the concerns expressed by the Commission who approved the plans for the school in September 1891 and told the governors they could now invite tenders for building.

There was a delay of more than a year before the governors eventually drew up the tender list in November 1892. The vendors of Upper Mall House had been proving difficult over the completion of the purchase. Almost another year elapsed before the purchase was completed in September 1893 and building operations could begin. At the beginning of 1893 the governors had accepted the tender submitted by W Downs in the sum of £10,200, which was £1,250 lower than the architect's estimate. Of the income available to the governors totalling £16,110, the cost of erecting the school accounted for £14,850. As well as the builder's tender of £10,200 and the purchase price for Upper Mall House of £3,000, there was £600 for school fittings, £800 for the architect's commission and contingencies, and £250 for the conveyancing involved in the acquisition of Upper Mall House.

The memorial stone was laid by the chairman of the governors on Saturday 9 December 1893 "in the presence of a large gathering of Ladies and Gentlemen". The chairman was Edward Bird, another member of the family

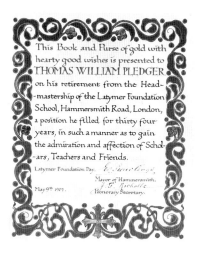

First page from the book presented to T W Pledger, Headmaster of the Foundation School, on his retirement.

Details of the opening ceremony of the new Upper School as recorded in the 1895 minute book.

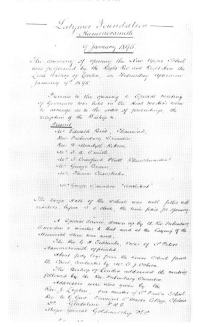

which had made such a sterling contribution to the Latymer Foundation over many years. A short service had been drawn up for the event and the choir was formed by senior boys from the Latymer Foundation School. The guests included representatives of the local councils, local clergy and the Surmaster of St Paul's.

Several months later, in July 1894, the board of governors held a special meeting to consider the scheme of administration for the new school and set fees at £5 a term. They took the first steps towards appointing a headmaster for the new school by approving a salary for the post of £120 a year plus capitation fees of £1 for every pupil (these, of course, did not last as the school grew in size). They also decided that they would consider only applicants aged between 25 and 32 who were Oxbridge graduates. It seems that the post was thus advertised but attracted an inadequate response. Accordingly, the governors readvertised the position in "the same papers as before" (that is, *The Guardian*, *The Athenaeum*, *West London Observer*, *West London Advertiser* and *Kensington Reporter*) omitting the condition and extending the deadline for applications from 1 October to 17 October.

At the end of October the governors short-listed 18 candidates from whom a final short-list of five was selected for interview. The interviews took place on 2 November at the Latymer Foundation School in Hammersmith Road. Ultimately the governors had to make a choice between two candidates: J Murray from the William Street Higher Standard Board School and the Revd C J Smith, the vice-principal of St Mark's College, Chelsea. The voting was seven votes to four in Smith's favour. It is said that the headmaster of the Foundation School, T W Pledger, expected to receive the post and that his failure to be appointed soured relations between the two schools for some years. Pledger's name was not among the five candidates short-listed for interview. This might be either because he never applied in the first instance (although his teaching record was a successful one and the Foundation School had been classed as a higher grade school since 1882) or because he lacked the qualification of a degree which the governors obviously regarded as essential for the post and which all the short-listed candidates possessed.

Ten days after C J Smith became the first headmaster of the Latymer Upper School, the school caretaker was appointed at £1 a week plus house, fuel and lighting, and a draft admission form was drawn up. At the beginning of December the governors heard that the Bishop of London, the famous Dr Frederick Temple (later Archbishop of Canterbury and father of the even more famous William Temple, another future Archbishop of Canterbury), had accepted their invitation to open the school, and they received a list from the headmaster of the assistant masters he had appointed together with their salaries and the forms for which they would be responsible:

1st assistant master	F Fowler	£160 pa	Form 4
2nd	D C Hutton	£150 pa	Form 3
3rd	S Pontefract	£120 pa	Form 2a
4th	W Eley	£110 pa	Form 2b
5th	J King	£105 pa	Form 1a
6th	H Butterworth	£105 pa	Form 1b

The 2nd assistant master, D C Hutton, had previously been on the teaching staff of the Latymer Foundation School.

On Saturday 5 January 1895 31 candidates sat the first Foundation Scholarship examination for admission to the new school. They were all examined by the headmaster in reading, writing, composition and dictation, arithmetic and algebra. The best 14 candidates were then further examined during 14–15 January in English grammar and literature, French, history, geography and Euclid. The headmaster marked all the papers and as a result the first five boys to enter the Latymer Upper School as Foundation Scholars, all of them having spent at least a year in a Hammersmith elementary school, were W F West, aged 12 (later to be a member of the Governing Body of Latymer Upper School), W J Mayer, aged 13, A D Tavener, aged 13, J Handford, aged 13, and W Pullar, aged 9.

The Latymer Upper School was formally opened at 3.00 pm on Wednesday 9 January 1895. Some 40 boys from the Foundation School again formed a choir for the proceedings. The Bishop of London referred blandly to the belief that "the well-taught man was likely to become a better citizen than the ill-taught man" during his discourse on "the Progress of Middle-Class Education in this Country", a title which firmly established the new school's place in English education's social hierarchy. Another guest, Professor Gladstone, reflecting the confused educational picture of the time, remarked that "The matter of secondary education was not properly understood but that defect was being rapidly removed". Altogether there were nine speeches on the occasion, with the chairman of governors, the headmaster, the two clerical governors, the local member of parliament and the Surmaster of St Paul's all making a contribution. The following Monday, 14 January, with the distinction of being the first pupil falling upon John Hodgson, the Latymer Upper School opened with 106 boys on the roll.

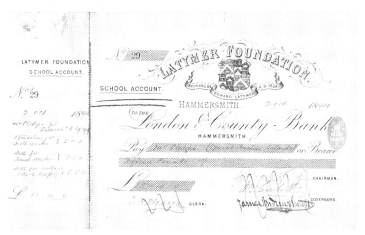

Cheque to Pledger, Headmaster of the Foundation School, for special teachers' salaries, 1894.

Latymer Upper School in 1915.

CHAPTER FOUR

'Spirit of Happy Good-Fellowship'

THE LATYMER TRADITION

1895–1919

The Reverend C J Smith was headmaster of the Latymer Upper School from 1895 until his retirement in 1921. He was a man of great character, vision and ability who quickly stamped his own personality upon the school. To establish the academic standing of a new school in so short a space of time and to sustain it for so long was an outstanding achievement. A good judge of men, he created within the school through his hand-picked staff a unique relationship between the boys and staff which was often remarked upon by visitors. A keen footballer and cricketer in his younger days, reputed for his underarm leg breaks, he did his best to promote a vigorous sporting life at the school quite often under considerable difficulties. Many schools claim one of their own for greatness as a headmaster. At Latymer Upper, the claims of C J Smith for this accolade can be taken seriously.

He was born the only son of a small tradesman in Hammersmith in 1854. After attending the school attached to the parish church and spending a year at the Latymer school, he began as a pupil-teacher at the St Paul's National School where he remained for five years. He was described as "a born teacher" with "a retentive memory and indomitable perseverance". During his time as a pupil-teacher, he was eager to continue studying and spent many evenings in the library at the South Kensington Museum, a walk of six miles each way. As a result of his studies he obtained a scholarship to St Mark's College, Chelsea, where he headed the list after the final examinations. He spent several years as an assistant master at the school attached to the college before being appointed headmaster of Cambridge higher grade school. Here he took the opportunity to enter the university as a non-collegiate member and he gained a first class honours degree in 1884. He also became an ordinand and was ordained in Ely Cathedral in 1886. He had left Cambridge the year before to become vice-principal of St Mark's where he remained until his appointment as the first headmaster of the Latymer Upper School.

At Latymer, where he was known as "C J" to the staff and as "Tubby" to the boys, he wanted to give an academic education to boys who would not otherwise have had the opportunity of one. He loved nothing more than to read out to the

Revd C J Smith, Headmaster 1895–1921.

Receipt for school fee for the first term of the first year, 1895.

assembled members of the school crowded into the school hall the academic successes of their fellow schoolboys. But he was equally proud not only of the achievements of the "cream" but also of those he termed the "milk".

He was a man of honour, integrity and great spiritual sincerity. He told members of the school's branch of the Scripture Union, which he was instrumental in starting, that they "must live up to their pledges. It was useless to join the Union if shady tricks were to be indulged in. The members must try to live quiet, straight and therefore influential lives".

He believed in the immediate despatch of discipline but he was always regarded as a very fair man. From the reminiscences of those who knew him, he comes across as a larger than life character. One autumn afternoon after school, for example, a boy was watching a football match in the school playground. While the game was going on at the other end of the pitch, he decided to relieve the tedium by climbing up the goal post at his end and swinging from the crossbar. "Suddenly I felt a terrific whack across the back and thinking it was a boy with a stick I called out 'Shut up, you silly ass!' only to receive another whack with a gruff reply 'I'll give you silly ass!'. I soon realised this was no schoolboy ... The sight of the portly figure in clerical frockcoat, bushy mutton-chop whiskers and rubicund face, topped by a round black felt old-fashioned clergyman's hat confirmed that it was 'Tubby' walking back to his home, Latymer House. I shinned down the goal post and was away like lightning to be well out of the range of the heavy brolly he carried." On another occasion, after completing a race on sports day, another boy took a short cut on his way home across an area of the school playing field which was out of bounds. Little escaped the headmaster's eagle eyes and he quickly gave chase as the boy took to his heels. Everyone else on the field at once stopped what they were doing to watch the pursuit. The cheering was loud and enthusiastic which only added to the head's turn of speed. The tails of his clerical frock coat billowing behind him, he shook his silver-mounted walking stick at his quarry, bellowing "You young devil, come here or I'll tan the hide off you", which, needless to say, he duly did. But the offence was always forgiven and forgotten once punishment had been handed out.

These stories show that even in administering corporal punishment he was no mean-hearted, steely disciplinarian. On the contrary, he was remembered for "his whimsical smile, ... his hearty grasp of greeting, ... his sound and lively speeches, enriched ... with humorous and apposite anecdote". This was a man who on a number of occasions lectured on humour to the school debating society which reduced several members to the verge of tears, so infectious was his own sense of humour.

At the time that the Latymer Upper School was opened, the development of secondary education was still in its infancy and there were very few trained teachers with experience of teaching at an advanced level. Nearly all of those available were elementary teachers, whose qualifications were usually limited to their teaching training certificates. It was thought unnecessary to possess university degrees for elementary teaching. Smith, however, had no doubts about the staff he appointed. He had trained several of them himself during his time at St Mark's College. Most of them at his request studied for and obtained external degrees from London University while they were teaching at Latymer. R C Davies wrote that "they were all good teachers and undoubtedly it was their pioneer work that gave the school that academic impetus that has remained to this day". Most of them remained at the school for the rest of their teaching careers.

Freddie Fowler was the first second master, a short, plump and serious man, who taught the senior boys and was responsible for many of the school's earliest academic successes. He served on the staff until his untimely death at the age of 55 during the post-war influenza epidemic of 1919. D C Hutton, known as "Bummy" because of his ample posterior, retired from the school in 1927. Walter Eley, called "Tim" by the boys from a tenuous association with a prominent Irish nationalist of the time, Tim Healey, was one of the trio of masters comprising himself, Pontefract and King who did much to lay down the school's sporting foundations. He retired in 1929. Jimmy King succeeded Hutton as senior master in 1927 and was the last of the original members of staff to retire, leaving the school in 1935.

Many of those who were appointed to the staff after 1895 also remained at the school until their retirement. Granville Morton Grace, who taught at Latymer from 1897 to 1929, was the first chemistry master at the school and one of the most brilliant of all staff to teach at Latymer. Known as "Cod" or "Coddy", he "peered through thick gold-rimmed lenses" and his "impregnated garments wafted a perfume of chlorine and sulphurated hydrogen with a dash of ether". Fred Weekes, who established the corps and developed rifle shooting at the school, spent 38 years at the school from 1897 until 1935. Edgar Coyle retired in the same year as Fred Weekes after 36 years at the school. It was said that he was appointed by Smith because he was such a beautiful singer. He made

Choir practice in the Great Hall, 1900s.

a number of early gramophone recordings and regularly had so many evening concert engagements that during the day he set work for his form to do while he caught up on his sleep. The Reverend Robert Palmer, otherwise known as "Beaky", and renowned for the severity of his marking, joined in 1899. One form's performance in a scripture test was resoundingly abysmal, with a single pupil managing to scrape a mere handful of marks. "Beaky", handing back the boy his papers, remarked dryly to him, "Taking up the church, lad?" Although he retired in 1936, he returned to the school in an emergency in the 1950s when he was a sharp as ever even though he was now in his eighties. C E Ayres, known to everyone as "Clem", was a fine Latin teacher, although he did not have a classics background, and he coached many boys to success in their entrance examinations for Cambridge. He spent 40 years at the school between 1903 and 1943, succeeding Jimmy King as second master in 1935.

The school had been open less than 18 months when its first inspection took place and the inspector remarked upon the "band of loyal, skilful and devoted teachers" which Smith had gathered around him. It was their "crusading zeal" which helped to secure a constant stream of academic honours and foster an esprit de corps often highlighted upon by inspectors. At the time many members of this devoted band not only worked together but lived together as well, Walter Eley, for example, recalling that in his early years at the school he had shared rooms on the Upper Mall with Jimmy King, Fred Weekes, Edgar Coyle, and Clem Ayres. The fact that so many members of staff served at the school for so long ensured that what the inspectors described as "a tradition of professional efficiency" in the school was passed on from one generation to another. Senior heads of departments came to exercise such effective supervision over their colleagues that it was said of the school that "service in it for a period of some years has proved to be in many cases a potent means of developing proficiency in the difficult art of teaching".

The head and his staff were supported by a sympathetic and tolerant board of governors. The head's requests for the appointment of additional staff as the school grew rapidly were nearly always granted. At a time when governing bodies did not always recognise the value of their teaching staff and often held their salaries down, the governors of the Latymer Upper School always ensured that their staff received salaries comparable with most teachers elsewhere. A particularly enlightened move was the establishment of a contributory staff pension scheme in 1912 which was superseded only when national superannuation arrangements were made for the teaching profession in 1920. At the time it was wound up it had become regarded as a model scheme and was emulated by many other corporate bodies. During wartime the governors never hesitated to award war bonuses to staff to compensate for the rising cost of living. A joint standing committee of governors and staff was established to meet once a term to discuss matters affecting the staff. The governors were generally receptive to plans proposed for extending the school to cope with increasing numbers. They were tolerant enough to admit a rabbi to the school to instruct the 23 Jewish boys on the roll in 1915. Almost without exception during the formative years of the Latymer Upper School, the board of governors, the headmaster, and the staff were pulling in the same direction.

The Latymer Upper School was not the only responsibility of the governors but it was probably the most important. The governors continued to take an interest in the running of the Foundation School although the school's management was now overseen by a board of managers under the control of the London School Board. The governors regretted that they lost even more say in the development of the school when the London County Council became the local education authority with responsibility for both elementary and secondary education in 1904. After the Upper School had been opened, the governors were also expected to implement the remaining element of the Charity Commission scheme and establish a girls' secondary school in the neighbourhood. During 1897 the Commission tried to persuade the Latymer Foundation to combine with the Haberdasher's Company and Aske's Charity to form a joint governing body to manage a new girls' school but all three rejected the idea. The whole idea was then put to one side until extensions to the Upper School were completed in 1900–1901. During 1901 the Latymer Foundation discussed the possibility of amalgamating with the trustees of the Godolphin School, the former boys' school which had closed in 1900. In the meantime the Foundation had already acquired a site for a girls' school at Lime Grove. The agreement reached by the two sides proposed that instead of a new school at Lime Grove, use should be made of the existing Godolphin School buildings. The Foundation would sell the Lime Grove site and put the proceeds plus an annual contribution of £500 a year towards the new scheme which would also include the Godolphin

King Street in 1910. The entrance to the school is on the right hand side of the road, with Rivercourt Methodist Church in the background.

47

Opposite page: *The Great Hall,
looking towards the organ and the
Memorial windows.*

endowment. The new school would be managed by a joint governing body. In fact the scheme was accepted by the Godolphin trustees only with some reluctance and largely because the Foundation was willing to lend them the considerable sum of £8,000 at a low rate of interest to pay off their outstanding debts and liabilities. The scheme was finally approved in 1904 and the school, known as the Godolphin & Latymer Girls' School, was opened on 1 March 1906 by the Duke of Leeds, the leading representative of the Godolphin family. The school has prospered ever since and has become one of the leading academic girls' day schools.

In the first years of the Latymer Upper School boys were drawn from a largely local area covering Hammersmith and Fulham and extending to North and West Kensington, Shepherd's Bush, Acton, Barnes and Brentford. Most commonly they had attended church schools, board schools or, of course, the Latymer Foundation School. But there were still boys who had never previously been to school at all, those whose early learning had been confined to home or private tuition, and those who had been taught by the elderly mistresses of the handful of surviving dame schools. In age they ranged from seven to 16 with half of all entrants being admitted between the ages of 11 and 13. Their backgrounds were mainly middle-class. A handful of fathers described themselves as gentlemen and there were some whose occupations conceivably placed them in the upper working-class, such as tailors, mechanics, gas engineers, and bootmakers. Largely, however, parental occupations encompassed the complete ambit of the English middle-class. On the one hand, there were salesmen, clerks and travellers, shopkeepers, grocers, butchers, drapers, and confectioners, publicans and wine and spirit merchants. On the other there were also architects, accountants, solicitors, insurance brokers, bank managers and directors, surgeons and dentists, art dealers, publishers and designers. One parent was an artist while another was an actress. Although, by the end of this period, more boys than before came from Middlesex and Surrey (37%), a majority still came from Hammersmith and the surrounding area (63%). By 1919 three-quarters of all boys in the school were aged between 11 and 15 but there were still 61 boys aged between nine and 11 and one boy who was under nine. Their social backgrounds at this time remained much the same. Labourers, artisans and domestic service accounted for 17% of boys' families. The rest were firmly middle-class, with 32% of families involved in trade, 23% with professional backgrounds, 18% employed as clerks or commercial agents, and 10% in public service.

One concern of the governors about the intake as time went on was that the numbers of boys entering the school from Hammersmith itself, not Fulham, Chiswick, or Turnham Green, but Hammersmith, did not increase in proportion with the growing total numbers in the school. Given Edward Latymer's original intentions, the governors had always sought to develop links between the Foundation School and the Upper School in an attempt to secure a sufficient intake of Hammersmith boys. Many of the brightest of the Foundation School's pupils, who were predominantly from lower middle-class backgrounds, regularly obtained places at the Upper School and the Foundation Scholarships helped many of those who would otherwise have struggled to attend. But it had not been an easy relationship because both schools took boys of similar ages. In addition 35% of the Foundation School's pupils did not live in Hammersmith.

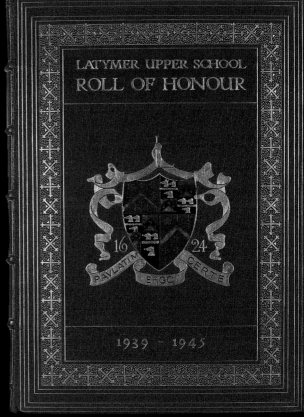

An attempt was made in 1903–1904 to link the two schools more closely. The governors were reluctant to see even more of their responsibilities for the Foundation School pass to the new education authorities created by the 1902 and 1903 Education Acts. It was suggested to them by the Board of Education that the two schools could become one under one headmaster, with the Foundation School acting as a lower school where boys remained until the age of 12 when they transferred to the Upper School. This idea was rejected by the governors partly because existing buildings were unsuitable for this purpose and partly because the Upper School was already taking boys from the age of seven onwards. Nevertheless the head of the Foundation School asked whether the curriculum of his school could be altered to prepare boys for the Upper School by the age of 11 while continuing to offer the existing curriculum for those remaining at the Foundation School until 14. This idea too fell on stony ground.

The idea was resurrected in 1916 when a special sub-committee was set up to investigate the admission of Hammersmith boys. It was reported that two-fifths of all boys who entered the school between 1909 and 1914 came from Hammersmith. The problem lay not with the entrance examination for preference was already given to Hammersmith boys who passed it. Rather it was attributed to the "unconscious, but not less real, rivalry between the Latymer Upper and a few of the Elementary Schools". The borough's elementary schools were not sending enough pupils to Latymer. Two reasons were put forward for this. Firstly, it was suggested that parents could not afford to send their sons to Latymer after they had completed their elementary education at 14. Secondly, it was also thought that the schools concerned were reluctant to lose their brightest pupils at the age of eight or nine. "What is really required", believed the governors, "is a Preparatory School for the Latymer Upper." This was an idea that the headmaster himself had advocated for some time although he had in mind an independent prep school rather than one linked to Latymer Upper. The provision of free elementary education had obviated the original purpose of the Foundation and the Charity Commission had always insisted that the largest part of the Foundation's income should be spent on secondary education. The governors were keenly aware that "the struggling clerk and the class who are obliged to keep up an appearance on limited means, many immediately above those who could send their children to council schools are very much in need of help, and we believe that Edward Latymer would approve of this view today". Now it was the governors who felt that the best way of achieving this was to create one school from the two Latymer schools, with the Foundation School acting as a prep school for the Upper School. It would ensure a better chance of historical continuity and lead to more Hammersmith boys attending the Upper School. The Board of Education, however, was no longer receptive to the idea.

In fact the school had never relied heavily upon the Foundation School for admissions. The closest links built up by the school over the years were with the education authorities of the Middlesex County Council and the London County Council both of whom directed an increasing number of their own brightest boys to Latymer Upper on county scholarships. Middlesex recognised Latymer Upper as eligible to receive its own county scholarship boys as early as April 1895. By the following October the first five London County Council

Opposite page (clockwise from top left): *Window on chapel staircase; the Isaac le Gooch memorial window; cover of the Second World War Roll of Honour; Frederick Wilkinson, Headmaster 1937–1957, portrait by Ruskin Spear RA.*

scholars were attending the school. In 1904 as a result of the 1903 Education Act which dealt specifically with London the education committee of the London County Council became responsible for administering both elementary and secondary education within its area and its ties with the school became even stronger. The Foundation invested rather more in the school each year than did the Board of Education and the direct grant from the LCC was much smaller than either of these contributions. But as the number of county scholarship boys at the school increased, so did the school's reliance upon the LCC for the greater share of the fee income it received. By 1919 out of a school roll of 664 boys, 28% held junior county scholarships while another 13% held scholarships from other sources including 44 with Foundation Scholarships.

The school quickly established an enviable academic reputation, at first principally for science but then also for the arts. The school had outstanding successes in the principal external school examinations of the time. These were the Cambridge Local Junior and Senior, but boys at the school also sat for the London Matriculation, those organised under the auspices of the Science and Art Department, and the commercial certificate examinations of the London Chamber of Commerce. When the commercial certificate exams were introduced in 1898, the school magazine, *The Latymerian*, urged Latymer boys to participate since the exams had been devised "in the hope of encouraging Commercial and Technical Education in which we are so much behind Continental nations". Boys already at school won the intermediate scholarships offered by the London County Council which assured them of a free education for 4 years. Pupils leaving the school at 16 shone in banking and civil service examinations while senior boys who stayed on at the school sat university entrance examinations. By 1900 there were some one hundred different examinations and the system was already under attack. It was accused of creating perpetual examination fever which resulted in pupils being unable to work without the stimulus of exams. The Science and Art Department was criticised for making its examinations part of the

The purpose-built chemistry laboratory of 1896. The school quickly established an outstanding reputation for science.

Left: *Under the watchful eye of the art master, 1910s.* Below: *an original repeating design drawn by a boy at a similar date.*

grant-earning machinery, but the payment-by-results system was only ended in 1904. The London Matriculation exam had never been intended as a school-testing exam. Only the Cambridge Senior was praised for the way it stimulated and guided pupils. In 1908 the Mayor of Hammersmith, speaking at the school's prize giving, remarked that "modern education seemed to be a turmoil of examinations and examinations were not education, they were really only a means of testing knowledge". The system was not reformed until the School Certificate was introduced in 1917. There was perhaps an element of truth in the criticism made by one Old Latymerian that the school before the First World War was run as an exam factory for turning out academic successes devoid of the social and cultural graces.

For some years the school operated its own payment-by-results system. Boys gaining honours in their examination results were each rewarded by the governors with a sovereign. Even those who passed obtained half a sovereign. No doubt this acted as an extra incentive for the boys to do well but the constant stream of good results from the school from the late 1890s onwards proved that there was more to it than that. In 1902 when the school's success in the senior examinations outshone the performance of all other London schools, the local newspaper observed that "Residents of Hammersmith are fortunate in having in their midst such an excellent school for the training of their boys". It was not long before the school was garnering an impressive list of university award winners. At the second inspection of the school in 1897, the first year in which the school had entered pupils for the Senior Cambridge examinations, the inspector had written that the school "had put within reach of all those who lived in the neighbourhood a good education for their boys. It gave a sound commercial education and more than that: he was firmly convinced that it was laying the foundation of an education which, for bright and intelligent boys, would find its full accomplishment in a University". This trend soon led to the alteration of the scheme of administration for the school to permit boys to continue their education up to the age of 18 without requiring the consent of the governors. One of the school's earliest successes was the achievement of the twin brothers, Mendel and Henry Trachtenberg. They had entered the school in 1896 from St Stephen's National School in Shepherd's Bush. One class-mate later recalled them as being brilliant pupils, difficult to tell apart, who knew all the answers and played piano duets together like angels in the lunch hour. In December 1900 Mendel headed the lists in the Cambridge Senior Local and won a mathematics exhibition to St John's College, Cambridge. In the following year Henry was awarded a subsizarship to Trinity College, Cambridge. They both enjoyed outstanding university careers. In May 1902, C J Smith, whose priority in his reports to the governors or in his public speeches was always the school's academic prowess, referred in his address at prize giving to the feat achieved by H H Mittell. Mittell, who had entered Latymer from Fulham Board School, had won an intermediate scholarship offered by the LCC while at the school, and had left to join the civil service before returning and winning an open mathematics scholarship to Cambridge a year later. In 1909 the school produced its first history scholarship winner, when C C Taylor won an open scholarship to St Catherine's College, Cambridge. In 1911 the school was awarded a half-holiday when G H Livens, who had left the school in 1906 for a place at Cambridge, was elected a Fellow of Jesus College and won the First Smith's Prize for his mathematics work. Another holiday was granted two years later when two other Old Latymerians and Cambridge graduates, H S Jones and T L Wren, were also appointed Fellows of their respective colleges. Jones became one of the school's most distinguished former pupils as Sir Herbert Spencer Jones, the Astronomer Royal. There were no student grants or student loans in those days. Thus the importance that was attached to scholarships and exhibitions which reduced the burden upon the individual student. The leaving exhibitions awarded to university students by the school also helped to make the difference between going up to university or not going up to university for some boys. By 1919 each boy leaving Latymer Upper for university was granted an annual exhibition of £30 a year for the duration of his degree course.

Most of the university awards gained before 1914 were for the sciences. The initial emphasis upon science in many secondary schools established in the late nineteenth century reflected the educational debate of the time. For many years there had been widespread concern at the inadequacy of science teaching and the fact that the country's primacy among industrial nations was now under serious threat. At the 1851 Great Exhibition Britain had outshone all her competitors in almost every department. At the Paris Exhibition in 1867 Britain excelled her rivals in only 10% of classes. Other nations had already established national systems of technical education or were in the process of doing so. A royal commission was set up to investigate the problem in 1872 in which year the Science and Art Department introduced Organised Science Schools, which had to provide a three-year course of instruction in a related group of science, manual and commercial subjects. Another important step came with the 1889 Technical Instruction Act which established local authorities for technical education, empowered them to raise a penny rate to fund it, and enlarged the scope of the Department of Science and Art. Many of the new secondary schools created from ancient endowments were encouraged by the Charity Commissioners to make provision for science.

The physics laboratory, 1900s.

At the Latymer Upper School this took the form of a purpose-built laboratory, a small step but one which would never have been considered at all 20 years previously. But the Foundation was so short of money after completing the building of the school that it could not afford to equip it. This was achieved only when the LCC Technical Education Board made a grant of £300 towards equipment as a result of which the laboratory was brought into use for the first time in June 1896. Annual grants were thereafter made at a similar rate by the TEB for the maintenance of technical instruction. Within a year there were 72 boys in three groups taking chemistry. Plans were already being made for a physics laboratory to accommodate the physics class that had been started, as well as for a workshop. The inspector who reported on the school in 1897 was very much in tune with the times when he observed that such facilities were essential since "science may be utilised to teach boys first to observe, secondly to enquire, thirdly to devise and finally to train their hands to execute what the brain has planned".

In 1897, to relieve the pressure upon existing staff, all of whom were responsible for a form within the school, C J Smith persuaded the governors to allow him to appoint the school's first specialist teacher to take charge of science. G M Grace was appointed to the post. It was a significant step. Grace was an outstanding teacher and the first one at Latymer Upper to prepare his pupils for university. Between 1900 and 1928 boys under his tuition gained a hundred university scholarships and exhibitions. He introduced a systematic course of science teaching and drew up the curriculum. He played a major role in the enhancement of science accommodation at the school. In 1901 new science rooms were opened which included a physics laboratory, a physics lecture room, a balance room, a woodwork room, and a new chemistry laboratory (the old one being converted into a dining room). Grace had designed the laboratories and super-intended their equipping, the latter again funded by grant-aid from the TEB. Grace bought drills, lathes and planing machines and made most of the physics apparatus to his own design. The new workshop, where woodwork classes began in 1902 under a visiting instructor, Mr Grimwood, also made apparatus for the physics department.

The Charity Commissioners insisted that the new accommodation could only go ahead if the school became an Organised Science School under the Science and Art Department. The initial reluctance of the governors was over-come when they realised that such status did little more than formalise the scheme of science teaching already being developed at the school for the senior boys and also brought the advantage of larger grants. The school's application was approved in 1900 by which time the Board of Education had taken over the responsibilities of the Science and Art Department.

In 1902 Grace was joined in the science department by G J Francis, known as "Georgie", who came with an excellent reputation from St Mark's Upper School. Like Grace, Francis too was a maths and physics specialist but he had taken chemistry as a subject for his second degree (he obtained a BA in 1894 in maths and classics and a B.Sc. in maths and physics in 1900, both from London University). It was for the development of chemistry that he was appointed. He was so thorough in applying himself to his task that before 1914 the science department was also sending chemists to Cambridge as well as mathematicians and physicists.

G J "Georgie" Francis, who joined the school science department in 1902.

Since the school received grants from both the LCC TEB and the Board of Education, both bodies undertook regular inspections of the school. Science teaching at the school came in for regular praise. In 1902 maths and physics were already regarded as excellent while the recent improvements made in chemistry were applauded. In the following year the TEB's Chief Inspector lauded the efforts of both Granville Grace and George Francis. There were now 162 boys in the three years which comprised the School of Science division and 38 of them were in the advanced division. Evening classes had been started for the brightest boys undertaking advanced work for the London B.Sc. or open university scholarships in natural science and mathematics and these were brought to an end only with the demands of the First World War. Arising from the recommendations of this inspection, another laboratory for advanced physics instruction was created from the conversion of a basement cellar in 1904. Six years later the tuck shop and bicycle shed were transformed into a modern physics laboratory. Visitors from all over the world were directed to the school by the LCC and the Board of Education since the quality of science teaching at Latymer Upper was held in such high regard.

During the 1900s the pendulum which had swung so firmly towards sciences and technical subjects during the late nineteenth century began to swing back towards the modern arts. This started with the Regulations for Secondary Schools issued in 1904 which recommended a curriculum which gave as much attention to English, history, geography, modern languages and Latin as it did to maths and science. The Regulations also recommended that only after pupils had been given a good general grounding in subjects should specialisation be permitted. This trend was reflected in changes at Latymer during this period. The modern arts side of the curriculum had not been neglected. For example, the teaching of modern languages at the school was well-regarded by inspectors although English reached similar standards only in the early 1900s. In 1906, however, the inspectors from the Board of Education were critical of the modern side of the curriculum, partly blaming the pressure of examinations. The report noted that "the literary side of the curriculum requires more time and attention. In planning a year's work a better graded and more suitable course of instruction could be arranged if less importance were attached to the supposed requirements of certain external examinations". There had obviously been insufficient progress by the time of the 1907 inspection when it was recommended that the school should appoint an English and modern languages specialist. Early in 1908 the governors agreed to the appointment as long as the person concerned also took responsibility for the upper forms in the school where numbers were increasing rapidly.

The man who was appointed was the Reverend Dr Edmund Dale, who had been a tutor at Chester Training College. He was himself a northerner, with a pronounced and rounded northern accent, and was by all accounts a dour, dry man. He possessed three degrees, all from London University, a BA, an MA in English, and a D.Litt. in English and History. He was not in fact the modern linguist the school had sought. He taught English, history and Latin to the Arts form he started on his arrival at the school. His doctorate had been awarded for a thesis on "Early English Life in the Mirror of English Literature" and he had a considerable love, enthusiasm and grasp of history which often made his sixth form teaching inspirational. Between 1908 and 1921 boys in the Arts form won 54 university scholarships and exhibitions in the subject. Boys in the form as well as scholarship work also studied for the London University Intermediate BA. This required five subjects, English, history, maths, French and Latin, to be taken during the course of a year and failure in any one paper meant resitting the entire examination. Dale established an Essay Period in which all three years in the sixth form (the third year being the scholarship year) met to hear one boy read an essay aloud which other boys would then be asked to criticise. Visitors witnessing this experience were always impressed by the boys' polished performance. It was so polished that one American visitor was convinced that it had all been rehearsed. With so much progress being made by Dr Dale, the governors then agreed to make a further appointment of a modern linguist, a recommendation made once again by the inspectors. In 1910 another highly qualified man, Dr E J Snee, who had spent many years teaching in Germany and France, was appointed to the post. In that year Latymer Upper could be counted among the schools alluded to by the LCC's divisional inspector when he wrote that "A number of secondary schools, especially for boys, which used to specialise in their higher forms in science and technology, are extending considerably the teaching of languages, literature and history".

While the school basked in the reflected glory of its university scholars, they comprised only a small part of the school and most boys left the school either at 14 or more usually at 16. The headmaster himself commented at prize giving in

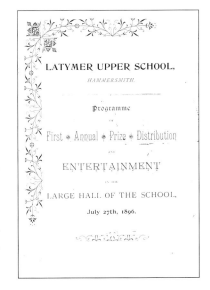

1911 that university scholars "were only the cream – what of the milk? The average boys were doing good work in bank, office, and business, and by this time were spread all over the world. Boys who went through the general education afforded had no difficulty, upon leaving school, in obtaining good appointments in these walks of life". As the concept of secondary education was developed during the period before the First World War, it was gradually accepted that the so-called secondary schools should cater not only for boys intending to progress to further education of some sort but also for those who would leave at 16. There was concern that the latter were not really being educated for the world of work, an echo of a debate which never seems to have been resolved. It was hoped that a common course of education for both types of boy could be offered although it was never very clear what that should be. As a concession towards commercial education boys in the early years of the school did have the opportunity to take shorthand and bookkeeping from the age of 11. But these were criticised as being a waste of time at school and more appropriately studied upon entering employment. They disappeared from the curriculum in the early years of the twentieth century after which all Latymer boys were taught a traditional array of subjects.

Each of these subjects (apart from a handful taught as optional subjects) was usually taught to the boys of any one form by their form master. Specialist subject teachers at Latymer before the 1920s numbered only a handful as we have already seen. Most of the early members of staff had been trained as elementary teachers and they were expected to be able to teach a wide range of subjects. For example, R C Davies recalled that when he was in form VI Mr Fowler, who was the form master, taught English, maths, geography, scripture, French, Latin and German to all the boys. Expected to teach his boys chemistry, Mr Hutton invariably practised the relevant experiment overnight but was never entirely free from nerves when it came to the actual demonstration. In the early years of the school the boys expected entertainment rather than education from their one lesson of practical chemistry a week. One old boy wrote that "a fine display of fireworks was expected. Should it not be of sufficient brilliancy, the poor pyrotechnist might possibly be pelted with pens and pencils by the disappointed occupants of the gallery".

For most of this period the task of form masters was made more difficult by the large size of many classes, and the mixed age range and ability of the boys in each form. The school grew rapidly in terms of numbers. By May 1896 the school roll stood at 350 and already exceeded the original capacity of the buildings. Applicants were being turned away in droves. The inspector from the Science and Art Department remarked that he knew "no other case of a school of a similar type (Secondary) filling in a year from the date of its opening". Still more boys were squeezed into the school but by the middle of 1897, when numbers were pressing 400, Latymer Upper was overcrowded. A year later and the governors' request to enlarge the school to a maximum of 500 places was approved by the Charity Commissioners. By 1902, however, the number of boys in the school had risen to 514. A new limit on numbers was set at 520 but they steadily crept up and up. Numbers remained below 600 until 1917 and by the beginning of the 1919 school year there were 664 boys in the school.

The school grew rapidly in terms of numbers ... applicants were being turned away in droves. School assembly, 1910s.

The school was always short of space throughout this period. Because of this shortage more boys were accommodated only because the size of each class was increased. Large class sizes and limited space placed great pressure upon staff. As early as May 1895 four of the six forms in the school were in excess of the maximum of 28, averaging 35 boys per form. Two months later, as admissions increased, the three lowest forms contained 38, 39 and 41 boys and the head was asking for more staff (one "to take charge of the backward little boys in a separate classroom") and more desks. The shortage of classrooms was also causing a problem during examination time. For five and a half days in June all boys not taking external examinations had to be sent home, much to parental irritation, since the noise from classrooms around the hall disturbed the concentration of the examinees. Another problem created by rising numbers was where to house all the boys' bicycles. In 1898 the governors agreed to construct more accommodation, including five new classrooms, and these were in use by the late spring of 1900.

Boys were moved quickly from one form to another to make way for the influx of new entrants, often as many as 10 boys in a form. They were already moved on a frequent basis since promotion from one form to another for many years occurred at the end of every term. Promotion was based upon the marks entered weekly by each boy into a journal which was signed by a master and then taken home for parents to scrutinise and sign. Forgeries were not unknown. The system had been introduced in the first place partly in order to keep track of the work of so many boys in each form.

Boys who did not reach the required standard at the end of each term were not promoted. Particularly in the fourth form this added to the problem caused by the inclusion of too many boys of varying ages and abilities. One Old Latymerian recalled that the fourth form room was always full since the form "contained a number of toughs such as Buck Bentley and Jack Hamnett who had no intention of going any higher and seemed to be there for life". It was always "the life-members in the back-row" who created the mischief "such as Johnny

Latymer Upper School
LITERARY AND
DEBATING SOCIETY,
SESSION 1917-18.

President:
REV. C. J. SMITH.

Vice=Presidents:
THE ASSISTANT MASTERS.

Hon. Secretary:
O. WOOD.

Hon. Treasurer:
E. F. BAXTER.

Committee:
C. A. WAKEFORD.   L. J. L. LEAN.
R. T. ATTRIDGE.   W. C. NORVILL.

SUBJECT.

Debate—"That a classical education is desirable."

Paper—"Old English amusements."

Debate—"That secret diplomacy should be abolished."

Paper—"Sir Humphrey Davy, Poet and Philosopher."

Debate—"That the pessimist is the true patriot."

Debate—"That present day literature has a just claim to immortality."

Paper—"Reminiscences of Germany."

Debate—"That war is a biological necessity."

Debate—"That all great men are bad men."

Paper—"Botanical Notes."

Paper—"Naval Occasions."

Debate—"That good government is no substitute for self government."

Paper—"Romanticism in English Poetry."

Paper—"The Five Declensions."

An early debating society leaflet, showing the remarkable variety of discussion topics.

Mahl, who sat behind us, [and] would take his icy-cold grass-snake from his pocket and wrap it around my neck! Those back-benchers would take it out of me if I so much as murmured".

Yet in 1905 it was the remove form, with 38 boys, which contained the smallest number of boys in the lower part of the school. The remaining eight forms for boys aged between 11 and 14 varied between 40 and 45 pupils. This was properly condemned by the Board of Education inspectors and in 1906 a further four new classrooms were built by extending the existing south corridor of the school. By 1909 the physics lecture rooms were being used as classrooms by forms of 28 and 30 boys respectively and work in a further two classrooms had to be restricted because of a shortage of space and lack of staff. One German class even had to be taken in the physics laboratory where there were no desks. In 1910 therefore three more classrooms were added. That, however, was the last extension of the school buildings before the 1920s despite an increasing number of boys. By 1919 forms below the sixth form still contained an average of 35 boys each while the school possessed only 19 classrooms for 24 forms. This left the senior science scholars without a classroom of their own and they were compelled to use the gallery in the gymnasium for housing their books, for private study, and for certain mathematics lessons.

Despite all this the teaching of boys below the sixth form received the support of successive teams of external inspectors. When the lower forms were examined by the Syndicate of Cambridge University in 1904, their work was found to contain "a high degree of excellence". In the following year the examiner from the Syndicate commented that examination successes of the lower forms revealed that "the task of keeping an efficient control of the written work of Forms of 40 boys is indeed accomplished" and that "the work of the school impressed me as in every way creditable".

One boy described the atmosphere of the school during the days of C J Smith as a "spirit of happy good-fellowship of which the Head was tutelary genius". Walter Eley recalled that in the school's early years the younger members of staff and the senior boys would get together for friendly evening entertainments in the school hall. During half-term Mr Palmer was known to take parties of boys on short cycling tours, for instance, to Windsor or Richmond and Barnes. The rapport between staff and boys was frequently commented upon by outsiders, even in days when discipline was much more rigorous and the gap between some teachers and their pupils could be awesome. In 1896 the school's first external inspector noticed that the boys and staff worked together as if they had been long accustomed to doing so. In 1901 the inspector was impressed with "the Tone, the relation between Master and Pupil being particularly good". In 1904 it was said that "masters and boys obviously co-operated with great heartiness and good will in performing strenuous and genuine work".

There may have been a spirit of happy good-fellowship but outside the classroom school life in those days was fairly austere. The first school society was the debating society which was not established until 1907. Topics debated by the senior boys covered everything from free trade and socialism to women's suffrage and blood sports. Perhaps the most remarkable debate was one in 1916 which proposed that kissing should be abolished when Wakeford's opening speech was said to reflect "many careful experiments" and "charmed the members by his lucidity and manly frankness". The motion was needless to say lost. A branch of the Scripture Union was formed under the charge of the headmaster in 1908 and the chess club was started in 1910. There were occasional lantern lectures on topics such as "British Colonies", "Across Canada in 1903", "Old Hammersmith", butterflies and moths, and tea planting in India. Until 1907 there was no school library as such, only the very limited subscription libraries organised by some of the forms. The school library was also narrow in its range, with an initial stock of only 300 books and very restricted opening hours. There was the usual criticism that boys preferred cheap literature to good books. Musical activity at the school began with the appointment of H Palmer to the staff in 1896 although this was largely confined to the occasional concert given during term by the school choir he formed and to the songs and musical pieces performed at the annual prize giving every year. As the school grew larger so prize giving was divided as early as 1897 into two with one for the upper school and one for the lower school held on separate days. In 1903, at the suggestion of one of the governors, Ascension Day was celebrated as Founder's Day by the school for the first time and for several years it was commemorated by organising a school trip for the boys. Empire Day was regularly celebrated from 1904 onwards with suitably patriotic songs and addresses and the saluting of the flag at a ceremony in the morning and a half-day's holiday in the afternoon. The school had a monthly half-holiday on a Wednesday afternoon. School visits and trips were rare. The King's Coronation in 1902 was celebrated when the boys from both the Foundation School and the Upper School were treated by the governors in July of that year to a boat trip to the mouth of the Thames. A special train was engaged from Hammersmith to Cannon Street from where the 850 boys and staff and 50 guests walked to the chartered steamer *Clacton Belle* which was anchored close by. There were very occasional theatre visits by groups of boys, like the fifth formers who saw Beerbohm Tree as Shylock in *The Merchant of Venice* in the West End in 1908 or the 180 upper school boys who visited the Benson's Company production of *As You Like It* in 1912.

There was no prescribed school uniform at first. A cap was the first item to be made compulsory and this was followed in the early 1900s by a school blazer and a school tie. The headmaster kept pointing out to the governors that the school had neither a motto nor a flag. It was only in 1911 that the Reverend Walsh, the Vicar of St Paul's and therefore a member of the board of governors, came up with the motto "Paulatim ergo certe" with its play upon the word "latimer".

Football was played with great enthusiasm by the boys from the time the school opened. It was characterised as "a game of skill" whereas rugby was simply "an exhibition of brute strength". The playground was the usual venue for the form championship which was fiercely contested. Complaints from neighbouring householders about the frequency with which balls appeared in their gardens led to wire fencing being erected as a preventative measure. In fact the playground was completed only in 1901 and during the 1890s was "a cindery Sahara in summer, which caked into a damp black surface in winter".

School football matches were played on the school field at Wormholt Park against teams from schools like St Olave's, Aske's, Emanuel, and Battersea

Programme for the 1913 celebration of Empire Day.

Boys in school uniform, sports day 1913. The uniform was introduced in the early 1900s.

An early Latymer Upper sportsman; G A Smith was Football Captain from 1897, adding Cricket Captain from 1898, and becoming overall Sports Champion in 1899 and 1900.

Grammar. Here also took place the annual sports day, first held in 1896. Wormholt Park was regarded as less than satisfactory as a playing field but it was tolerated on the grounds that Latymer Upper was a new school, space in London was limited, and at least it was flat! In the summer of 1901, however, notice to quit what was known as "Wormholt-cum-piggeries" was given to the school. For the footballers the field which belonged to the trustees of the Godolphin School was rented but that was unsuitable for the cricketers who had to wait until 1902 before a suitable ground was found for them at Barnes. The annual sports day was transferred to Stamford Bridge. In 1905 the governors purchased a 10 acre playing field at Wood Lane which has remained the school ground ever since. It took until 1908 for the ground to be properly prepared and drained so school matches still had to be played elsewhere. Wood Lane is not ideally situated and it has been criticised for being too small but attempts to sell it and secure something better have never yet succeeded.

The popularity of the annual sports day ebbed and flowed according to the degree of enthusiasm of each generation of schoolboys. In 1913 the school sent a team for the first time to the Public School Sports without success, but in the same year won the Inter-School Sports, competing against Emanuel, Wilson's, and Aske's. The following year 250 boys were transported to the same competition at Herne Hill in an "imposing procession of motor buses" where the school swept the board to the accompaniment of "the inevitable awful 'Rah! Rah! Latymah!'" In 1916 the school did win the Public School Sports Challenge Cup and all the boys were granted a holiday the following day.

Cricket was well-supported and matches against other schools and colleges, like Rutlish, Camberwell Green, St Mark's College, and the Foundation School, were arranged each year. The ground at Barnes, a large field behind the rectory, was very pleasantly situated. But it was too far from the school for evening matches and the man looking after the field refused to cut the grass except in the immediate vicinity of the pitch – the "tall waving grass in the foreground proved a very effective deterrent to high scoring". So it was used for one season only and for the lack of a suitable ground cricket was abandoned at the school for the next five seasons until a better field was obtained. When cricket was revived, the boys were excused their homework for one night each week in order to encourage cricket practice.

A swimming club was quickly established at the school. The school competed against other schools regularly. Boys from the school attended swimming lessons three times each week at the local Hammersmith baths and once a year staged a school swimming gala which other boys and parents were welcome to attend. From this stemmed the long tradition of water polo at the school. Hammersmith baths became increasingly unsuitable for the boys as more and more wanted to attend swimming lessons. In 1908 the 300 members of the club began using the modern baths which had been built at Lime Grove on land that had been sold to the local authority for that very purpose by the Foundation. In 1914 the strength of swimming at the school was such that at the London Secondary Schools Association annual competition Latymer Upper came away with 18 medals and the competition shield, which the team had the pleasure of receiving from their headmaster, who was the current chairman of the association.

For a school which backed on to the River Thames any participation in rowing was largely confined to viewing the Boat Race each year from a specially erected grandstand in the school grounds. The boys did row on the river during the early years of the school but only on a casual basis and rowing was abandoned in 1904 because of lack of interest. The formation of a tennis club was proposed by Dr Dale in 1909 but thrown out by most other members of staff as too lightweight a sport for boys. Boxing on the other hand, which was only started at the school in 1907, flourished for more than 20 years. All this sporting activity took place either outside school hours or on Saturdays for the timetable never included games afternoons.

A gymnasium was built at the school during the programme of building work which was completed in 1901. Gym classes were introduced, as in so many other schools, in response to the debate that was raging about the fitness of the nation's young men, given the wayward campaign that had been fought by the British army in the Boer War. Sergeant Major Wood was the first instructor and annual gymnastic displays were held from 1904 onwards. In the same spirit a non-uniform cadet corps was established in 1905 under the command of Colour Sergeant Fraley, thanks largely to the determination of the only female member of the governing body, Mrs Cresswell. Drill was taken regularly and in 1909 the corps obtained Martini–Enfield carbines with the pins removed to replace the wooden dummy rifles with which they had previously practised. A miniature rifle range was built along one side of the school in the summer of 1907 and opened with great ceremony by General Sir John French in January 1908. Poignantly in the light of later events, Sir John told the assembled boys that the range was significant because it reminded them that their primary duty was to prepare themselves to take their share in the defence of the Empire. The rifle club became very popular and boasted 250 members by the summer of that year.

Boxing in the playground, about 1910; a sport which flourished at the school in the early decades of this century.

The gym after 1901.

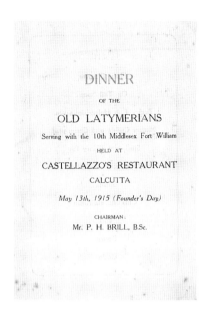

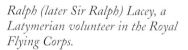

The links between the old boys' association and the school were close. The association was founded with 30 members, each paying a subscription of 3s. 6d., on 5 February 1897. Originally it was known as the Latymer Old Boys Association, but this was subsequently changed to the Upper Latymer Old Boys Association in 1898. The association then requested and was granted permission to use rooms in the school every Friday evening for their meetings. Among the activities which the club organised were chess, draughts, boxing, a Christy Minstrel troupe, swimming, rowing (although, like the school's rowing activities, this was also abandoned in 1904), bicycle rides, tennis, and roller-skating around the hall and along the corridor. Lectures and discussions were also held. In 1900 the inaugural annual dinner was held at a restaurant in Holborn and in 1902 the association gave the first of its annual concerts. Recent leavers were encouraged to join on the basis that, since Latymer was devoted to "the production of commercial men", the older members could help younger members to find positions in the world of commerce.

It was the often devastating losses among old boys that made the First World War so traumatic for many boys' schools. At Latymer Upper nearly 300 Old Latymerians had already joined up by the autumn of 1914. Several members of staff had also left for war service. Temporary staff were recruited in their place but their posts were kept open for them until they returned and the governors agreed to make up the difference between their army pay and their normal salaries. Sergeant Major Wood had rejoined the Gordon Highlanders and Colour Sergeant Fraley was training young officers at the Inns of Court Officers' Training Corps. Older boys were training in their spare time and the school was already welcoming several displaced Belgian children to its ranks. The first Old Latymerian to be decorated was F F Pullen in December 1914. He received the Legion of Honour for repairing an aircraft while under fire and bringing it away with the pilot. In the same month the first Old Latymerian was killed in action. Sergeant R F C Yorke died near Ypres on 22 December 1914. He had been an outstanding athlete at school, becoming a well-known miler and half-miler, and had represented Great Britain at the Stockholm Olympics in 1912. He had taken charge of a captured machine gun post after the death of his commanding officer but "a German bullet caught him full in the forehead and so caused the death of a thorough sportsman and a gentleman".

At first the contributions to the school magazine from Old Latymerians serving at the front were tinged with optimism and the excitement of their first experience of military action. They contained no hint of the bitter misery of the later years of the conflict. For example, Norman Wright, who was later killed in action, took part in the extraordinary Christmas truce that occurred in December 1914. He described how lights appeared along both trenches on Christmas Eve and each side shouted the compliments of the season to the other all night, singing and applauding in turn. On Christmas Day both sides left their trenches and met in the middle of no man's land, shaking hands and swapping hat badges, buttons, and cigars. "I shall be quite sorry to have to fight these [men]", he wrote, "for I feel sure that they are quite all right and only the victims of unfortunate circumstances." Another old boy, J McLeish, serving in the London Scottish, wrote that "Dodging shrapnel is certainly exciting and

Ralph (later Sir Ralph) Lacey, a Latymerian volunteer in the Royal Flying Corps.

amusing at times; it's when one gets hit by it that the fun ceases". In 1915 boys who had been in the previous year's fifth form were now serving at the front and that year's Vb remarked that "if the war keeps on, some of us will be able to send a thrilling account to be put in the Magazine".

It did not take long before attitudes changed. Senior boys began to find it difficult to concentrate upon their work as the trickle of old boy fatalities became a steady flow and so many of their friends on active service were now in constant danger. This was in sharp contrast to the younger boys who remained more brazenly patriotic and had little comprehension of the horrors of war. The optimistic poems contributed to the school magazine in the early days of the war gave way to more sombre verse such as the anonymous poem entitled "Latymer's Dead" in July 1917 whose first verse ran

> Like ruthless hands that clutch a blushing rose,
> Grim Death has crushed them fiercely in his rage;
> Laughing, they lived a bright day to its close,
> Then died, to sleep untroubled for an age.

Latymerians in the First World War.

School life began to change in small ways as the war progressed. Economies had to be made as the LCC reduced its annual grant. Swimming and the annual sports day were abandoned. Life saving was dropped in favour of more drill. Many cricket matches were scratched because opponents were having to attend cadet corps drills. Certificates replaced prizes at the annual prize giving. The burden upon staff increased as more and more of their colleagues joined the forces. The choir came to end when Mr Waddams, who conducted it, gained his commission. The evening classes in advanced science ceased when Mr Grace began to use the time to help make aircraft engines instead. Mr Eley took over

Opposite page: *The squash court, once owned by the author Naomi Mitchison.* Inset: *One of the many decorative animals added by her to the original building.*

three acres of the field at Wood Lane to grow vegetables and parties of boys went on harvest camps. The debating society was temporarily suspended because of lack of interest. Prefects were appointed for the first time in 1915 to assist with the running of the school under the circumstances. The headmaster reported to the governors at the end of 1915 that "The war has taken away all boys of 18 and the chance of well-paid employment in Banks etc. has tempted away from school many much earlier than they would have left in peacetime". In 1916 the non-uniform corps became a properly organised and officially recognised uniformed cadet corps under the command of Mr Martin. In 1917 it numbered 10 officers and 347 boys. During late 1917 and early 1918 German air-raids over London and the rumour of air-raids interrupted the regular attendance of many boys.

The first memorial service, sombre, dignified and proud, for the growing number of the school's dead was held at Hammersmith parish church in February 1916. When the second service was held on Ascension Day in 1917, the number of dead had more than doubled and there were over one thousand old boys involved in active service. The regret at the passing of those who died before reaching their prime was heartfelt. The dead included "perhaps intellectually the most brilliant boy that has passed through the school" as well as "one of the finest all round athletes the school has had". One particularly poignant casualty was Mendel Trachtenberg, one of the school's earliest university scholarship successes, who died from malaria contracted while on service in Egypt and Palestine in October 1918, less than a month before the end of the war. Two brothers, G H Heavers and C A Heavers, were both killed in the same action on the same day. 216 Old Latymerians lost their lives during the war out of 1,234 who served. The headmaster keenly felt the loss of all these boys but suffered his most grievous loss through the death of his own son. In May 1919, as the school began the task of returning to normal, seven ex-servicemen returned to school to resume their studies in VIIa Science.

CHAPTER FIVE

'Wise Conservatism'

THE INTER-WAR YEARS

1919–1939

C J Smith wanted to see the school through the first few years after the war. He had been expected to retire in 1919 but the governors were more than delighted for him to continue as headmaster. Gradually school life resumed its normal pattern. Boys, masters and Old Latymerians returned from the war, all of them marked for ever by the experience, and some of them completely broken by it. Memorial tablets recording the names of the school's war dead were erected in the hall and funds subscribed towards an organ in their memory. The corps struggled in peacetime, much to the head's regret, for he believed in "the permanent value of this training in the formation of character by discipline and self-control". Prizes were awarded once again at the annual prize distribution and concert. The debating society recycled old debates. School sport flourished, particularly football, swimming and athletics. Pressure on space remained acute since the school was as popular as ever. In 1920 there were 348 applicants for admission of whom only 29 were admitted. In the same year 26 Old Latymerians were in residence at Cambridge. A fellow headmaster wrote to Smith, who was President of the Incorporated Association of Headmasters of Secondary Schools that year, saying that it was simply too much for him "to walk off with 75% of firsts in a Tripos at Cambridge".

Changes were fairly minor. Under Dr Dale, an advanced evening institute was opened at the school for local people to attend. Chemistry facilities were improved by the conversion of the existing dining room into an improved laboratory and balance room. After discussion with the prefects, a house system was introduced at the school. Restricted purely to sporting purposes, it divided the school into six houses, each with a house master, house prefects and house colours and named after historic Hammersmith houses. It was well-received. Within two hours of the announcement the first primitive house ballad was being heard. One youngster told his house prefect that "You ought to be jolly thankful you've got me in your house".

Smith announced his intention to retire at the end of the 1920–1921 school year. The final school inspection during his term of office undertaken by the Board of Education took place in March 1921. Some of the inspectors' recomm-

Field Marshal Sir John French at the school to open the 1914–1918 War Memorial, 1921.

endations followed the pattern of the past. There was a need for more classrooms, the unsatisfactory use of the gymnasium and gallery had to be resolved, a dining room should be provided for boys who presently ate their lunch either in classrooms or in Ravenscourt Park across the road from the school. They were critical of the junior school, made up of the first four forms in the school, which they felt to be lacking in "the brightness and keenness that should characterise it". They recommended the appointment of an assistant master especially to take charge of this part of the school.

Of the curriculum the inspectors reported that

> The high standard in Mathematics and Physics has been maintained while the standard in Chemistry has been raised to the same level as Physics.
>
> At the same time under the inspiring control and guidance of the chief History Master the literary side of the school has developed until it is of equal importance with the scientific side and as well regarded in the school.

They noted that the strength of the school in these areas meant that other subjects were often under-regarded. While applauding the recent appointment of a specialist geography teacher, they were critical of the standard of Latin and German and of the lack of emphasis given to craft work and physical training. But to dwell on these points is to cavil. Overall the inspectors were immensely impressed with what they found at the school. They reported to the board of governors that "the work accomplished at the school was of a very high order and the discipline excellent, and the good feeling which existed between masters and scholars was remarkable". The final sentence of the formal report read: "To the retiring Headmaster the contemplation of the school as he leaves must be a source of pride and satisfaction".

It is possible that the governors were swayed in their choice of a second headmaster by the inspectors' suggestion that he should be selected with a view to strengthening the literary side of the school. Initially the governors had wanted to limit applications from those aged 48 or under but the Board of Education

Cambridge Latymerians' Social, 1929. A large number of boys from the school went to Cambridge in the post-war period.

had objected to this since it ruled out applications from senior masters at the school. The governors changed their mind which enabled them to appoint from a shortlist of seven applicants Dr Edmund Dale by nine votes to four.

Dr Dale was in the tradition of many headmasters of his time. Although he was known as "Daddy", he was remote, aloof and austere. His duties as headmaster greatly curtailed his teaching and few boys ever saw him other than collectively two or three times a day when he conducted assemblies in the morning and afternoon and on his way to and from lunch. Emerging at precisely ten minutes to nine each morning from Latymer House, the head's house at the far end of the school grounds, he made his stately progress through the playground and the long school corridor towards his study, all activity ceasing as he reached each part of the route, the boys parting like waves as the head came through. He was completely imperturbable. On a rare occasion when he was a few minutes late, one boy was caught unawares playing with a ball in the corridor as Dr Dale entered through the swing doors. The boy froze, the ball dropped from his hands and bounced desultorily down the corridor towards the approaching headmaster. Without interrupting his stride the headmaster silently swept up the ball and strode onwards. It was an impressive performance. A similar happening occurred one summer afternoon when the headmaster was returning from lunch. One boy playing cricket in the playground had picked up a ball close to the boundary and hurled it with all his might towards the wicket when he suddenly realised that the respectful pauses in other games indicated that Dr Dale was passing by. He watched with horror as the ball sped towards the headmaster and hit him neatly in the stomach. He stopped and the boy hurried towards him, anxious about the possible punishments which might befall him. The boy having stammered out his apologies, Dr Dale merely remarked very scathingly that if the boy could not manage to throw a ball straighter than that, he had better not throw at all!

Even Dr Dale's prefects rarely saw him. One boy received his prefect's badge in a state of terror from Dr Dale who, failing to pin it to his jacket, said in his rounded northern vowels "Here you are, you'd better have it, off you go, well done!". The prefect concerned never saw his headmaster to speak to again during the whole year.

Dale was firm and strict. He insisted upon politeness, courtesy and obedience from his boys at all times. The seven school virtues he considered to be "quietness, steadiness, manliness, duty, honour, right, godliness". The disdain he felt for anything less than proper behaviour was economically expressed in one edict which addressed the boys' conduct upon the railways: "They should not attempt to travel in first class carriages with third class tickets". Boys found in possession of *Wizards*, *Hotspurs*, and other weekly comics had them confiscated and were given a stern lecture by the headmaster. He frowned upon poor timekeeping and detested untidiness which led him to develop in the early 1930s "a scheme of uniform clothing for boys attending the school as is the custom in all the best schools". One lady in Rivercourt Road once reported two boys for failing to wear their school caps, providing the headmaster with yet another occasion for an admonitory lecture to his pupils. He was never very interested in younger boys and could be cruelly unsympathetic at times. One young scholarship boy from a poor home was sent by his form master to receive the head's

Revd Dr Edmund Dale,
Headmaster 1921–37.

Dr Dale in the headmaster's room, 1923.

congratulations upon his position as top of the form. He returned not beaming but crestfallen. The only words that Dr Dale had spoken to him were "Your nails are unclean!" But he was never a martinet. He viewed the use of corporal punishment as a regrettable necessity which was to be used only "with discretion and should not be excessive". This stricture was perhaps not zealously adhered to by the prefects whom one former pupil recalls as administering justice "rather liberally". Dr Dale preferred to demonstrate corporal punishment as an example to others. When a number of boys were caught stealing, they were publicly caned by the school caretaker, under the eagle eye of Dr Dale, in front of the rest of the school at assembly one morning. With his staff he could be autocratic. Unsolicited comments from staff at common room meetings were usually met with the phrase "I presume, gentlemen, you are not criticising me!" The saying was that there were only two infallible men in the world: the Pope and Dr Dale. He kept parents at arm's length. They were welcome to make an appointment to see him but "indiscriminate interviews" were not permitted. They had to earn his respect and he could be witheringly scornful of parents with unrealistic expectations of their sons' abilities. Dr Dale confessed on one occasion to the governors that "Sometimes I tell such a father bluntly that his son would never matriculate if he stayed at school until he were 70". Although he could be narrow and unimaginative in outlook, he was nevertheless a generally fair man. He was consistent in his decisions, always adhered to what he said, and displayed a tolerance and lack of prejudice that belied his manner.

For Dr Dale what he termed "the Spirit of Work" was paramount. "In all school activities", he said, "work takes precedence." He scrutinised rigorously academic performance throughout the school. Any sign of slacking was likely to prompt a stern memorandum from the headmaster to his staff outlining the failings he had detected and the action needed to rectify the situation. He had little time for boys who left school before their time or for those who had done nothing for the school and he was irritated by the presumption on the part of most boys that a testimonial from the headmaster once they had left would automatically be forthcoming. "Those boys", he wrote, "who are so steadily neglecting Home Work and doing nothing in school organisations can find their testimonials where they have been spending their time to the detriment of their school duties and loyalty." He passionately believed, as he emphasised when addressing the school in 1927, that "a university career is the natural crown of a secondary education ... No boy, provided that he had the two essentials, brains and character, could afford to neglect, nor could his parents afford to neglect for him, the happiness, the culture, the wider interests, and the increased opportunities that a university education could give".

The hallmark of Dr Dale's era for many boys was that "Everything was geared to passing exams". A boy's performance was judged almost entirely by his examination results. Such inflexibility led on at least one occasion to boys with a record of excellence in a subject being denied the chance to study it in the sixth form because they had failed to pass the relevant examination at a lower level. But Dale maintained with considerable success the remarkable academic record which had been set by his predecessor.

The first Oxford award gained by the school came in 1925 when T H Simms won an open exhibition in history to Merton College, Oxford. Typical of the results of this period were those for 1928. In the General School Certificate examinations, 45 boys matriculated, 28 gained certificates, and 13 honours and 103 distinctions were recorded. In the Higher School Certificate there were 17 successes with four distinctions. There were seven awards to Cambridge, one to Oxford, and 102 other university successes. In 1933, when the seventh form (which we would now call the sixth form) contained 63 boys studying maths and science and 43 studying modern languages, literature and history, the Board of Education inspectors spoke of the school's "high reputation for vigorous post-Certificate work", a reputation which since the school's earliest years had attracted and continued to attract dozens of overseas visitors directed there by the Board of Education and the London County Council.

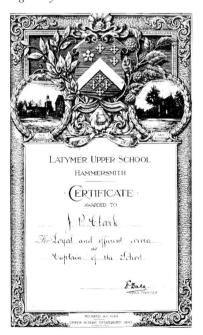

Certificate for loyal and efficient service as Captain of the school, signed by Dr Dale.

This academic success was based upon a continuation of much of what had gone on in the time of Dr Dale's predecessor. Dr Dale himself had taught at the school since 1908 and many of his staff had served there even longer (the *average* length of service by staff in 1921 was 14 years). If what had gone before had proved to be successful then there was little appetite for changing it among the great majority of staff who knew no other way. Although the introduction of the School Certificate made a coherent programme of work possible for the first time in both the first five years of the school and in the sixth form, the bias of the curriculum remained heavily in favour of the sciences, English, and history. Other subjects, like a second foreign language, geography, music and craft work, continued to be under-taught. This was made worse by the fact that the school week contained five fewer periods than most other schools. Boys were still promoted on a termly basis, a system now openly criticised as old-fashioned and disruptive. This led to a widely disparate group of boys coming together in the year in which they sat the School Certificate – in 1933 the inspectors found that this year group of 100 boys contained 44 who had reached this stage in less than four years, 24 who had taken more than four years, and only 32 who had taken the prescribed four years. The inspectors also found that the curriculum was too heavy for some less able boys. This resulted in 41% of all boys who left the school after the age of 14 departing without taking School Certificate. Given the school's overall record, however, which was always acknowledged by the inspectors, Dr Dale felt able to exhibit a robust disregard for the latest advice being offered by educationalists. Towards the end of his time, in December 1934, he wrote that "We have our own ideas and our own ways and do not fit in exactly with the usual administrative or educational plans of the secondary school system … our theories are thoughtful and sound, our work is consistent and good, and at the same time as proof we have excellent examination results to show".

Outside the classroom things also remained much the same. The house system flourished and was extended from sport to other school activities. All the usual sporting activities continued, with house competitions fostering a keen sense of rivalry among boys. Every Saturday seven or eight school teams played football and in addition there were the house competitions, junior football, and games for non-players. The soccer competition was held during the winter in the playground where matches were played in the lunch hour. Playing on the asphalt helped to teach players to stay on their feet while the absence of touch-lines and the element of chance from the posts supporting the netting above the side walls made the pace fast and furious. Those who kicked the ball over the netting, however, were sent off. In the summer the playground was host to many scratch games of cricket, each using a tennis ball, with wickets chalked on the side walls. A similar penalty as in the football matches was employed for hitting a ball over the netting of "six and out". Many a game came to a premature end when a culprit failed to obtain any answer to a knock on the door of the house where the ball had landed in Weltje Road or Rivercourt Road. Swimming was particularly strong and boasted nearly 400 members in 1924. The school repeatedly recorded sound performances at the Inter-Schools Sports and Public School Sports. There were attempts to revive rowing but Dr Dale was never enthusiastic. But only the first two years in the school were given any games coaching or instruction and then only on one afternoon each week. It was still believed that by the third form each boy would know which sport he wanted to follow and therefore "need not be given extra time for them in school hours".

Dr Dale at cricket, about 1927.

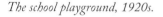

The school playground, 1920s.

Sport in the 1920s at the school's playing field at Wood Lane. Above left: *Dr Dale umpiring cricket.* Above: *Keen spectators.*

The chess club was successfully re-established. Bible classes took the place of the long defunct Scripture Union. Here, and in the meetings of The Seekers, established by Dr Dale in 1934 to discuss religious subjects from a scientific point of view, the Latymer spirit of tolerance was encouraged through a vigorous exchange of opinion about modern views of the Bible. On the other hand, the library was still open only to those who paid an annual subscription of 6*d*., contained very few books and even fewer of real interest to the boys, and was used by only one-third of the school roll in 1933. Rifle shooting remained very popular, much to the occasional discomfort of residents in Weltje Road who complained of the odd stray bullets from the rifle range shattering house windows. In those days school shooting matches were played by post. Both sides would shoot on the same day and post their targets to the other side. This arrangement permitted Latymer Upper to engage in matches with schools as far away as South Africa. The corps survived the post-war reaction against all things militaristic by becoming a band of 150 keen volunteers rather than 600 often unenthusiastic conscripts. For these keen recruits, the corps provided opportunities for specialising in signals, for playing the bugle or drums in the band, for first aid and nursing, for shooting with small bore rifles, and for a fortnight's annual camp during the summer holiday. Founder's Day, whose celebration had fallen into disuse, was revived and Empire Day continued to be celebrated,

The rifle range, 1920s; rifle shooting remained very popular at the school.

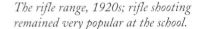

1930 Latymer contingent of the OTC marching to attention on Marlborough Down.

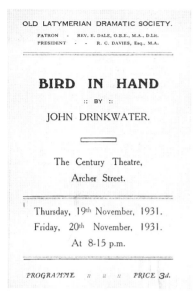

OLD LATYMERIAN DRAMATIC SOCIETY.

PATRON   ·   REV. E. DALE, O.B.E., M.A., D.Lit.
PRESIDENT   ·   ·   R. C. DAVIES, Esq., M.A.

BIRD IN HAND

:: BY ::

JOHN DRINKWATER.

The Century Theatre,
Archer Street.

Thursday, 19th November, 1931.
Friday, 20th November, 1931.
At 8·15 p.m.

PROGRAMME :: :: :: PRICE 3d.

Programme for a play by the Old Latymerian Dramatic Society. The Old Latymerians became very active from the 1920s onwards.

although with less and less enthusiasm as the years went by. The annual prize giving continued in its time-honoured form, with the distribution of prizes punctuated by items of music and drama.

The old boys, who changed the name of the association in 1928 to the Old Latymerians' Association, resurrected the weekly Friday evening meetings at the school and these continued until 1939. During the 1920s the association became much more active, particularly in terms of sporting activities. For many years old boys had played football together on various grounds through a club called the Sutton Court Football Club, although it was not restricted to Old Latymerians. After the death of C J Smith, funds were subscribed to acquire a sports ground for the old boys in memory of the school's first headmaster. In 1928, for £3,200, a ground was purchased at Whitton Park, Twickenham. The problem was that there was insufficient money left after the purchase to pay for its preparation and then its upkeep. Many old boys gave up their time to fill in the moat that ran the whole length of the field, to fell trees, to level and seed the ground and build a perimeter fence. The task of filling in the moat, which required two thousand tons of soil, was not completed until 1950. The first game was played at Whitton in 1928 and it was decided to erect a purpose-built pavilion and clubhouse to replace the temporary structures then in use. This was financed through a company set up for the purpose, Whitton Park House Ltd, which issued debentures to raise the necessary cash. Subsequently, once the debentures had been paid off, the ownership of the building was returned to the Old Latymerians' Association. As well as football and cricket, the association also formed a golfing society in 1936.

The determination of Dr Dale to plough a lone furrow if necessary as far as the academic management of the school was concerned and the retention almost intact of a pattern of activities which had been established largely before the war might lend weight to what *The Latymerian* described as Dr Dale's "wise conservatism". Yet innovations were introduced during his headship and there were indications that he wanted to do much more than he actually achieved. At the end of 1922 the head wrote that he was convinced that there was "a New Spirit abroad". But there were several constraints upon the development of this new spirit.

Firstly, the inter-war years were difficult ones financially for the school. In the summer of 1921 the governors had been concerned that expenditure was outstripping income and several plans were deferred. They were compelled to raise fees in the autumn to £16 10s. a year but new pupils who joined the school from outside the LCC area in future were to be charged £31 10s. a year (subsequently subsidised by Middlesex County Council to the tune of £10 per pupil). Only three months later, however, the governors were faced with a reduction of 10% in the grant they received from the LCC which was forced to make cuts in spending because of the difficult national economic situation. The LCC was urging all secondary schools to make a similar cut in their own expenditure. Many schools reduced the number of teaching staff. Latymer was hardly in a position to do this since it had only 32 staff compared to the recommended staffing level of 38. Instead, in 1922, the LCC made a unilateral decision to reduce the salaries it paid to 20 of Latymer's staff by 10%. The staff protested strongly to the board of governors who agreed wholeheartedly to forward their protest to the LCC but it was some years before the cut was restored. At the school the governors forbade another increase in numbers until further notice. Detailed departmental budgets were presented to the governors for the first time and every item of expenditure came in for eagle-eyed review. The governors seriously queried the request made by the headmaster for more desks (there were too many boys for too few desks). This drove Dr Dale to give a stern warning to the governors that there were certain fundamental items which could not be neglected. Then there was the perennial question of additional accommodation. Dr Dale repeatedly pressed the governors to sanction more new classrooms from early 1924. The governors duly applied to the LCC who repeatedly refused to provide the necessary funds until the middle of 1929. Similarly the wall intended for the front of the school as part of the Tercentenary Celebrations in 1924 was also deferred until 1929. In that year the governors wanted to purchase 235, King Street to create more space for the school but the LCC refused to allow the Foundation to purchase the property. The Literary Evening Institute, one of Dr Dale's brainchilds, provided a variety of courses for local people aged over 18 and was still flourishing in the late 1920s, with 375 members on roll in the spring of 1928. In 1929 it was shut down by order of the LCC to save money. Then came the Depression. Further reductions were made in the LCC grant, including another 10% cut in teachers' pay. Nevertheless the governors refused to raise fees since such action might have prevented boys continuing at the school and they did so only in 1932 at the behest of the LCC.

The second constraint was the long service of many of the staff. The headmaster may have been autocratic in his relationship with them but he knew that old dogs could not be taught new tricks. That was why, as many of them retired in the mid-1930s, he encouraged their replacements to make their mark. In March 1936 he issued a staff memorandum which went as follows:

> The Headmaster hopes that the newer and younger members of the Staff will not delay to make full use of the opportunity to put life in to the school sports and all games. The large number of new appointments makes the point that there is a large room and opportunity for fresh blood in many directions. As the Spring draws on he would like to feel the actual reality of the presence of a youthful and vigorous Staff.

The third constraint was more intangible. The comment above shows that Dale recognised the need for change that only an infusion of new blood could bring. He knew that the world was changing and, as he showed in his report in December 1935, he was not unsympathetic to such change: "Education is coming to the dividing of the ways and seems to be heading for a much wider expansion in scope and opportunity. ... Boys have changed greatly since the war and seem now to be setting their faces to work out new ideals with something of a new purpose and a new spirit". There again, 13 years after he first used it, is that little phrase, "a new spirit". But Dale recognised that he too was one of the "old dogs". The full range of changes, that he perhaps wanted to introduce and encourage but which he perhaps recognised he was temperamentally incapable of achieving, would have to wait for another man.

That is not to belittle the changes which did occur. There were many small changes. Attempts were made on several occasions to establish a school orchestra, all with limited success. A field club for nature study was started. Senior boys enjoyed discussion, lectures and rambles. On one ramble to Ruislip in 1927 "an old gentleman threatened to give us in charge for loitering with intent to steal his water-cress, but he forgot this and was soon arguing vigorously with our Chairman on the war in China". The introduction of biology to the curriculum in 1927 led to an influx of applications for membership of the club. A separate science library was opened and soon afterwards the Science Circle, a group for senior boys which arranged science lectures and visits to places of scientific interest, was set up. A branch of the League of Nations Union was established in 1933 with more than 50 members. It seemed that the greater the disaster which befell the League of Nations itself during the 1930s then the greater the attendance at the Latymer Upper branch of the Union. In 1932 Dr Dale finally got his own way and a school tennis club was established with 22 members which used the Ducane Road hard-courts "as well as the alleged grass-court on our own ground".

Dr Dale often encouraged staff to have their heads. The two most innovative changes of the time came about because of this. In 1928 Mr Longland, Mr Blades and Mr Davies took 39 boys during the first week of the summer holidays to stay at a college at St Germain-en-Laye, 15 miles from Paris. There were two organised excursions, otherwise the boys were free to choose their own itineraries, "even including the Moulin Rouge". From then on until the outbreak of war in 1939, the school took parties of boys abroad every year. Germany and Switzerland became particularly popular places to visit in the years which followed. The rise of Nazism made little impact upon the boys during the German tours of the 1930s. They recorded what they saw in matter-of-fact terms, the Nazi uniforms everywhere, the swastikas and portraits of Hitler, the rare political discussion they had with German contemporaries. Dr Dale was, however, very sensitive about the boys' visits to Germany. The school magazine for 1934 contained a cartoon by one of the boys entitled "The Swastika Bird". The headmaster took the view that this might cause offence and imperil that summer's forthcoming German trip. On his orders, all copies of that issue were piled upon the piano in the hall and the offending pages torn out and destroyed.

Right: *The first school trip, to St Germain-en-Laye in 1928, and* (below) *an original receipt to a boy for £5 15s. 6d. to pay for the excursion.*

74

It was under Dr Dale that one of the most striking characteristics of the Latymer Upper School for many years was first established. F J Skinner came to the school in 1921 to occupy the position Dr Dale had held before he became headmaster. Skinner stayed only until 1927 when he left to move to Runcorn Grammar School as its headmaster. At the end of the Christmas term in 1921 all members of the sixth form met under Mr Skinner's chairmanship to discuss whether or not to revive the moribund debating society. Instead it was decided to begin a literary, musical and dramatic society run along the lines of a similar society Mr Skinner had known as a student at Reading University. This itself had been based on the medieval craft guilds. In January 1922, the temporarily elected committee of this new society met in the gymnasium with the headmaster in the chair. The society was to be known as the Gild. It was to be run by a small committee known as the Curia. The headmaster of the school would always fill the post of Custos while staff would also take the roles of Reve and Steward, roles which always proved central to the vibrancy of the Gild. Boys filled the remaining roles of clerks, cofferer, public orator, searcher and forward-mannus. Other posts were subsequently created. Members of the society, who were restricted to the sixth form, were to be called Gildani and each Gildanus had to swear an oath of initiation upon enrolment: "I promise to labour always for the Common Weal, the increase of Humayne Lerninge, the honour of this School, and the fair fame of our Gild". Once a Gildanus, always a Gildanus, even after leaving school. The Gild would meet every Friday evening after school and such meetings were to be known as morowspeches. The final morowspeche in each term was to be a Gild Entertainment. Eventually this performance came to be known as the Jantaculum and was given at the end of the Christmas term. The very first morowspeche took place at 4.00 pm on Friday 20 January 1922 when 66 Gildani were enrolled. The minutes of the Gild meetings, known as the Chronicles, recorded "Thus and thus was our Gild established; and every gildanus returned to his home that night blithe and hopeful in spirit".

Part of the purpose of the Gild was not only to replace the debating society with a forum for broader activities, but also to bring members of the arts and science sixth forms closer together and build closer links between pupils and staff. The morowspeches, usually well-attended, included debates, play and poetry readings, lectures, and musical evenings. In 1924 one debate voted overwhelmingly for the introduction of rugby to the school since football was now "tinged with professionalism". This was regarded as "a valuable indication of the feeling in the school" but nothing came of it. 1924 was also the year of the Tercentenary and the morowspeches were temporarily abandoned while Gildani rehearsed intensively for a full scale dramatic production, the school's first, as part of the celebrations. *Henry V* was performed to acclaim in February 1925 but it was noted that "we must guard against the Gild's being turned into a society for producing one play a year, which is against its aim of broadening our artistic horizon by regular periodical doses of drama, music and literature generally". Interest in the Gild was so keen throughout the school, despite qualms from time to time about poor attendances, that a Junior Gild, providing a similar range of activities, was established for the fourth and fifth forms by popular demand in late 1924. When the Apprentices was formed along the same lines in

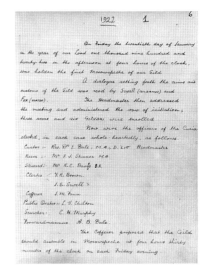

The Gild. Top: *First minute of the Gild, 1922.* Middle: *Archie Davies, the first Reve, here seen teaching English.* Bottom: *The first Curia of the Gild.*

The 1930s. Above left: *the opening of the Grand Pavilion at Wood Lane, 1933.* Right: *Sir William Bull MP, a governor of the school, at the opening of the Memorial Gates of Ravenscourt Park, 1933.*

1937 for the second and third years, almost the whole school had the opportunity to take part in Gild activities. There is only one recorded instance in these early years of a Gild member being expelled. In January 1926 the Chronicles recorded that "The name of H G Jones was deleted from the roll of Gildani on the 29th day of January 1926 because he had broken his Gild vows by malicious interference in the lighting arrangements of the Jantaculum and refusal of an apology".

Dr Dale was able to say to the Gild in September 1924 that already "our Gild was becoming a great force in the life of the school". By the time of the 100th morowspeche in 1927 it was recorded that the Gild "has grown to be an essential part of school life, whose vigour is more astounding by comparison with the decadence of the Debating Society which preceded it. It has developed a tradition so strong ...". Thus there was little danger of the Gild collapsing when Mr Skinner left in 1927. On the contrary, in the hands of R C Davies as Reve, the Gild went from strength to strength.

As far as he was able, under the financial limitations of the time, Dr Dale also sought to "soften and humanise" the school buildings in line with the new spirit which was abroad. Stained glass appeared in the windows in the hall. Prints were hung in the redecorated corridors. With persistence, other parts of the school were gradually improved or extended. In 1931 the new classrooms which the LCC had first been asked to fund in 1924 were finally completed, creating a new library, art room and geography room. An adjacent property was acquired to house the caretaker and provide two small dining rooms for boys. The caretaker's old quarters became a biology laboratory, the old art room was turned into a more comfortable staff common room, and the prefects were given their own room in a small former classroom. The old cricket pavilion, infested with rats, was at last replaced in 1933. In 1934, after months of negotiations, the governors agreed to buy 239, King Street and 61, Weltje Road, next door to the school. This block of property, which became known as the New Building, was converted during 1936 to provide a new larger dining room, an improved biology laboratory, and a music room, all of which had been recommended by the inspectors from the Board of Education in 1933.

As in the past, new buildings were required partly because of the increasing number of boys at the school. From 664 pupils in 1919 the number of boys rose to 777 by the end of 1936. Primarily because of its academic reputation the school was very popular with parents within the school's catchment area. Latymer's intake did not greatly alter although there was an increase in the number of boys entering the school from Hammersmith. In 1921 26% of pupils came from Hammersmith, 34% from other London boroughs, 32% from Middlesex and 8% from Surrey. In 1933, the percentage of boys from Hammersmith had risen to 31% and from other parts of London to 37% at the expense of boys from Middlesex (30%) and Surrey (2%). The main reason for this was the differential in fees between those set for boys attending Latymer Upper from within London and those for what were known as out-of-county boys. Despite the increase in the number of Hammersmith boys, the governors always felt that greater efforts should be made to increase it. Again the idea of using the Foundation School as a prep school for the Upper School was mooted. Discussions never got very far although the governors stated that "this question was of vital importance that the two schools ought to be linked together and that the matter ought not to be lost sight of". As far as scholarship pupils were concerned, Dr Dale followed more generously the pattern set by C J Smith and each year the number admitted averaged 35% of the annual intake. In fact, in 1933, the inspectors found that 45.1% of the boys at the school were exempt from fees.

Dr Dale retired in 1937. He had always wanted to see a chapel at the school and had pressed hard to no avail for one to be provided for the Tercentary Celebrations in 1924. Now he found his opportunity and as his final legacy to the school the Chantry Chapel was installed in an empty room at the top of the New Building and consecrated by the Bishop of Kensington in July 1937. But Dr Dale left far more to the school he had served for 29 years. Most importantly

The school in 1935.

*Frederick Wilkinson, Headmaster
1937–1957.*

of all, perhaps, he had continued to foster the Latymer spirit so firmly established by C J Smith. One old boy from this period described the characteristic Latymer boys of the 1930s as conventional but not unimaginative, assertive without being aggressive or bossy, competent rather than brilliant. Latymer's tolerance and liberalism inculcated in boys the ability to respect another point of view while not necessarily agreeing with it and a broadmindedness which would not put up with nonsense. Latymer boys of Dr Dale's day most certainly were not produced in a rigid mould.

Dr Dale's successor was Fred Wilkinson. Aged 46 at the time of his appointment, he had been educated at Dudley Grammar School. He had then taught for four years, including two under the famous Sanderson of Oundle, before entering Sidney Sussex College, Cambridge. His studies were interrupted by the war during which he served in the infantry and in the air force as an observer and attained the rank of captain. His wartime experience profoundly affected his outlook on life and "imbued him with a deep belief in the importance of international understanding". Returning to his studies after the war, he graduated in history in 1920. Subsequently he became senior history master at Liverpool College before being appointed headmaster of Wallasey Grammar School in 1927. He remained there for seven years, establishing a reputation as one of that school's greatest headmasters. Enthusiastic, persuasive, without a trace of pomposity, he was an excellent selector of staff and took a particular interest in music and drama which flourished at the school. He established links between the school and the Schadowschule in Berlin which lasted until the Second World War. He introduced rugby and ensured that the school's rowing club was well-provided for. He left Wallasey in 1934 for the headship of the Regent Street Polytechnic School. He spent only three years there before applying for the Latymer post, telling the governors that he found that "the many other activities of the Polytechnic leave very little scope for the development and improvement of the boys' school". His appointment as the third headmaster of the Latymer Upper School rested, it was said, upon his assertion that the first thing he would do would be to start a rowing club at the school.

"Wilkie", as the new head became known, was a very different man from his predecessor. He was the dividing line between the old and the new for many boys. Those who knew Mr Wilkinson only during their final year at Latymer felt far more familiar with him than they had ever been with Dr Dale. He was more approachable, more humane, more sensitive, more imaginative. His authority as a headmaster, which he always retained, came not from a remote aloofness but from a quiet dignity. His instinct was always to put the interests of the boys first, a habit which could be irritating when he would suddenly break off a conversation with a member of staff to talk to the boy who had just knocked on his study door. This was never intended as a slight, it was simply the way he was. Like C J Smith, he was a headmaster with a remarkable memory who knew the boys and their backgrounds. An idealist and a visionary, he could be vague, unpredictable and inconsistent. A very emotional man, he was easily moved to great and affecting eloquence which occasionally became long-windedness and sentimentality. Morning assemblies often ran well over time which annoyed staff waiting to teach their first period of the day and was not necessarily appreciated by the cramped masses in the school hall. At ease when speaking with boys, he often found it difficult to find the right level of communication with their parents. With staff he never shirked from making his points with forcefulness but he was prepared to listen to their comments and opinions and, if necessary, to bow to their judgement.

Although he never forbade corporal punishment, it was something he himself used only with reluctance. Boys despatched to the head's study by staff rarely returned with a beating but nearly always came back with a contrite heart after the most effective verbal admonition delivered quietly but firmly. He developed this style of discipline to a fine art. On one occasion while he was standing in the hall three senior boys passed by him on their way to their common room five minutes after break had ended. The head did not know that all three had a free period and, with a sideways glance at them, his watch in his hand, he said "Really, you know, you fellows, you leave the rest of us to run the school and you are late". Such was his personality that all three boys immediately felt guilty of an offence they had not committed and protested in chorus "But sir I'm free!" Wilkinson replied at once that he was sorry. Then with impeccable timing as the three boys left the hall, he added "And what's more I'm sorry I'm sorry".

It was later written of Mr Wilkinson that under his headship "one witnessed the transformation from a Grammar School of high academic reputation and achievement but one at which examination results and University successes were the top priorities, to a school where these things still counted for much but became secondary to the building of a school where a boy's individual needs and his relationship with his fellows mattered most". He believed in the whole boy, the all-round boy, and was not prepared to extol only the brightest and the best. For some of those who had taught at the school under the unbending academic regime of Dr Dale, this change was difficult to accept.

But in the main this and the many other changes which Wilkinson intended were welcomed and supported by staff at the school. The last of the original members of staff had retired in 1935. Several others went in the remaining years before the war, including "Georgie" Francis, the senior chemistry master, who was known to be out of sympathy with the changes which were being made, Henry Janau, the geography master, and E C "Froggy" Longland, who had been in charge of the junior school for many years. The other more senior members of the common room generally proved to be more receptive to new ideas than their immediate predecessors. These included men like R C "Archie" Davies, the small, enthusiastic English master and energetic Reve. "His gleaming dome, his bushy eyebrows, ... his spry, alert figure and his wonderfully nasal intonation (imitated by thousands of Latymerians) are unforgettable", recorded *The Latymerian* in later years. From him many boys learned to enjoy the treasures of English literature. A colleague in the department was the brilliant but self-effacing A E M Bayliss, known as "Bill", who wrote more than 40 textbooks and was a prolific author of one-act plays. Some of his verse was set to music by Eric Coates and through his membership of the Savage Club he brought figures like Walter de la Mare to the school. Another notable English master was "Bunter" Sutton, who taught literature and later went on to write novels of his own. With his expressive readings and thorough explanations, he instilled a sense of drama

H V Janau was head of geography at the school from 1921–38.

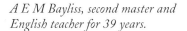

A E M Bayliss, second master and English teacher for 39 years.

A D Sopwith, senior history teacher, 1927–53.

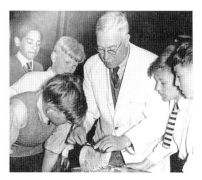

"Treacle" Treacher, who ran the workshop.

David Charles McIntyre, a long-standing head of art.

into many boys. There was A Blades, the lively German master, who pioneered foreign tours at the school. E D Goddard and W "Dogsbody" Wheatley were stalwarts of the chemistry department. A D Sopwith, whom the boys called "Beery" for obvious reasons, ran the Junior Gild as well as teaching scholarship history with great success. Art was never taken seriously at the school until David McIntyre was appointed in 1927 to run the newly opened art room. He was a multi-talented man, a skilled etcher, water-colourist, fabric designer, letterist and bookbinder. Mr Treacher, who went under two nicknames, "Knackers" or "Treacle", ran the workshop for many years. Many new members of staff had been appointed during the 1930s. They were of a different generation of schoolmasters, friendlier, warmer, more informal. "Monty" Cann, the first school chaplain, joined the school in 1935 to teach English. An excellent teacher but a stern disciplinarian, he professed to be an aggressive philistine, littering his criticism of musical events with phrases like "gut-scraping", "caterwauling" and "highbrow nonsense". Wilf Sharp came to the school as a young man to teach English in 1937 and brought a sense of fun and liveliness to his teaching which enthralled all the boys he taught. G A Wiggans, appointed to take charge of PE in 1931, was a man of genial disposition but one of the loudest voices boys had ever heard. Years of shouting at boys in the gymnasium must have taken their toll for he seemed to be incapable of saying anything quietly. George Offiler and F G Gregory joined at the same time in 1931. George Offiler carried on the excellent reputation of the Latymer history department. Gregory, who became known for his frequently used dismissive exclamations, was a talented linguist, who led many of the school's overseas trips and later introduced Russian to the curriculum after the war. Dr Eric Briault, who later became Chief Education Officer for ILEA, came to teach geography. One boy later recalled that for the first time geography "was not just maps and rivers and places. He spoke to us of economics and trade and crops and climates".

As promised, one of the first things Wilkinson did was to establish a school rowing club. In early 1938 the Furnival Sculling Club had offered the school the free use of their boats and premises in connection with National Fitness Week. Wilkinson had accepted with alacrity and in March rowing recommenced at Latymer for the first time in 34 years. Dick Southwood, an Old Latymerian who had won the double sculls title with Jack Beresford at the 1936 Olympics, kindly gave his assistance. On 4 March 1939 the school won the first race held against the Polytechnic School by one and a half lengths. A further change soon followed when the organisation of games was altered to provide every boy in the school with physical exercise at least once a week. All forms took either football or PE with rowing and tennis as optional choices for older boys. Distance running was encouraged by the introduction of the round-the-river course in March 1939 along the banks of the Thames, over Barnes Bridge and back via Hammersmith Bridge, which created Latymer's own cross-country course in the heart of London. In the same year the school also started its own scout troop.

Prize giving became speech day at the end of 1937 and was divided into three parts for the senior, middle and junior school because of the large number of parents who had to be seated in limited accommodation. The junior speech day became the first official parents' day. Intended to bring parents into closer contact with the school and cultivate the relationship between parents and teachers, parents were invited to tour the school and talk with the staff. The headmaster signalled his intention to start a parents' society to foster these links between home and school. The celebration of Founder's Day, which had once again fallen into abeyance, was revived in May 1939 and held in the school hall.

There were other plans afoot. It was intended that the junior school should become a separate institution from September 1939 by installing it in the former headmaster's house, Latymer House, with Mr Bayliss as headmaster. The governors noted that "The separation of the Junior boys will undoubtedly be a good thing for the school and will provide an immediate remedy for the congestion of the school's accommodation". The work was intended to take place over the summer holidays. In preparation for this the head had taken the step of appointing the first woman member of staff, Miss Parry-Okeden, to teach the lowest form in the junior school. This was viewed by some governors as "a revolutionary step" over which they felt they should have been consulted.

At the same time there were serious discussions about the provision of "adequate and modern accommodation for the present needs of the school and … for its future development". The governors fully accepted the criticism of the school buildings made by the LCC inspectors. They drew up a list of improvement schemes, including the provision of completely new buildings which they recognised could not be implemented without considerable grant-aid. They discussed but ruled out the idea of completely rebuilding the school on a new site for the sound reason that this "would have unforeseeable effects on the character and traditions of the school". But they did recommend that, rather than piecemeal rebuilding on the present site, the school should be rebuilt on that part of the site nearest the river. The sale of the site on which the existing school buildings stood would raise funds for the new school and it was expected that both the LCC and the Board of Education would be willing to fund the difference. Detailed plans were to be prepared in the expectation of making a start in 1942. With this strategy the LCC were in complete agreement. More immediate events, however, were soon to throw any plans the headmaster and governors may have had completely off course.

Revd Monty Cann, the school Chaplain before and during the Second World War.

Governors planting trees at the Wood Lane sports ground, 1926.

CHAPTER SIX

'Decency, Tolerance and Kindliness'

THE SECOND WORLD WAR

1939–1945

The imminence of war brought boys back to school earlier than expected after the summer holidays in 1939. The crisis was handled with the same level-headedness, good organisation and pride with which the school had prepared for evacuation during the Czechoslovakian crisis in the autumn of 1938. When school was recalled on 25 August 1939, 110 boys and four masters had already departed for Queen's College, Taunton, under a private scheme which had been previously arranged. Over the next four days masters and boys returned to Hammersmith at short notice from their summer vacations. Among them were the sons of German refugees who been fortunate enough to escape from the country while there had still been time. Several boys travelling abroad had exciting tales to tell of their return journeys. For many of them the impending war seemed to have little personal relevance. Among the party of Latymer boys touring Savoy that summer, "everyone was almost wholly oblivious of the gathering storm". One sixth former, returning on 1 September from an international summer course at the university of Freiburg, spoke of his companions, but not himself, when he wrote "What a pity they'll be knocking merry hell out of themselves in all too short a time!" At the school the growing band of pupils whiled away their time playing organised games in the late summer sunshine until plans for the evacuation had been finalised.

On Friday 1 September 1939 at ten minutes past three the school was evacuated. A party of 550 people, which, as well as Latymer boys, included some sisters and brothers and a few mothers, trooped to Ravenscourt Park station to catch the Richmond-bound train. They were only a small part of a massive effort over a period of three days which resulted in the evacuation from London of nearly one and a half million people, most of whom were children. At Richmond the Latymer party caught the Southern Railway service for Windsor from where they were ferried by a series of buses and coaches to villages in the countryside surrounding Slough. The school was divided into five groups. 250 boys in the charge of Mr Jackson were taken to Gerrard's Cross, which became the school's temporary headquarters. Mr Clewley took 160 boys to Iver Heath. At Richings Park there were 60 boys with Mr Fowles. At Horton and Farnham Church there

Opposite page: Preparation for the 1938 evacuation.

The 1939 evacuation – Latymer Upper boys disembarking at Windsor railway station.

were two parties of 20 boys each accompanied by Mr McIntyre and Mr Goddard respectively. By six o'clock everyone was settled into their billets for the night. The impeccable Latymer organisation had survived intact the attempts of energetic policemen and officious railway personnel to disrupt it.

"For us", wrote one boy, "the big adventure had only just begun; this was the greatest thing that had happened in the lives of most of us, a sudden journey to an unnamed place, strange people, and a different home, a home established to suit the needs and comforts of some other family quite unknown." The newcomers received a warm welcome into the homes of their willing hosts but took time to realise that their presence was a constant intrusion upon the lives of those who took them in. Boys were sometimes too independent when help should have been sought, indifferent when assistance was required, too clever to be kind. There were inevitably cases where boys were unhappy or behaved badly in their new homes. Monty Cann, who was based at Richings Park and kept a record of the first few weeks of the evacuation, noted on 21 September that "Several complaints are beginning to come in as foster parents get used to the boys and the novelty wears off. These cases are all visited and the people seen as well as the boys as time permits". But there were many instances where boys settled in well and formed relationships with their foster families which outlived the war. One local boy in Iver regarded the 13-year-old Latymer boy who stayed with his family as an elder brother who made model aeroplanes for him out of balsa wood and took him on fishing trips. Another Latymer boy who joined the same family, the son of West Indian parents, and the first West Indian boy to be seen in the neighbourhood, always kept in touch with the family after the war. Latymer evacuees generally soon became part of the small communities where they were living, mixing happily with the local children. Games of cricket were often played between teams of Latymer boys and local boys in those "warm and providentially dry September days". The match against Iver boys ended with each side indulging in ginger beer and cakes.

No permanent school accommodation was found for Latymer Upper until the beginning of October and in the meantime staff had to make their own arrangements. A degree of central control was exercised over the outposts by a messenger service from headquarters at Gerrard's Cross. At Richings Park, this was regarded more as a hindrance than a help. Within a week of the evacuation, staff at Richings Park formally recorded their view that "it would be conducive to the better running of their district if HQ staff were kept at HQ. There is overmuch petty interference". Largely, however, staff at each location were left to their own devices. At Richings Park the boys were divided into three groups based on age. Roll call was held each morning at 10.00 am and boys were expected to attend in uniforms and caps. The day was made up of two sessions, from 10.00 am to 12.30 pm and from 2.00 pm to 4.30 pm. Prayers were said in the local church after roll call every morning. Under the instruction of Mr Sharp, the boys made harnesses and water-proof containers for their gas masks and cleaning squads were formed. For the first two weeks or so, the sessions at each location consisted of a mixture of lessons in first aid, sewing and drill, organised games and walks. At Gerrard's Cross the sixth formers had the privilege of playing tennis against the girls of Maltman Green School on the latter's courts and defeating them. At Richings Park the Latymer boys arranged a football match against evacuees from Stepney who were also billeted locally. The day before the match the Latymer boys began to mark out the pitch. "When they returned to complete the job after lunch", Monty Cann recorded, "their Whitewash had been utilised by the Stepney evacuees for purposes of political propaganda. 'Down with Hitler' was painted all over the pavilion and the pitch was marked with noughts and crosses!" The Richings Park contingent also formed a concert party, known as "The Latymerryuns", which gave a series of concerts written, directed and produced by Wilf Sharp and Monty Cann. They took the show to Horton where a hall filled almost entirely by boys from Stepney heartily booed the chaplain when he appeared on stage dressed as Hitler under the name of Herr Adolfo Benito.

On Monday 18 September the various groups were sufficiently well organised to commence schooling proper. Books and equipment had been ferried bit by bit from Hammersmith on the return journey of the local market gardener's van from Brentford market, although staff did not always receive what they asked for. At Richings Park Mr Waddams was seen to be "gloating" over the discreet removal of chalk from one local school and a blackboard from another. Unconventional premises were obtained. At Richings Park lessons were held in the Congregational Hall. It was reported that Mr Logan "seemed so pleased at getting a class together for the first time that he refused to break and continued in defiance of the timetable and to the disgust of his class for two periods". At Gerrard's Cross the boys were taught in the local pub, "The French Horn", where the penny barrel organ was always ready to provide a loud musical accompaniment for the least liked lessons.

Then on 27 September a message was despatched from the headmaster informing all groups that the school would reform as a whole on Monday 9 October at the girls' secondary school in Slough. It was now that the senior boys rejoined the school from Taunton where they had spent a miserable month, apparently largely living off plain bread and mustard and cups of cocoa, alleviated only by the plentiful swimming, football and cricket played throughout September's wonderful weather. The scheme fell through when the regular boarders returned. Unlike many other schools, which often had to share school premises, Latymer had full-time use of the Slough school. 564 boys were housed in buildings which had previously accommodated 300 girls. Only the lower forms were short of a full timetable, and then only by three periods a week which were given over to extra games. An efficient canteen was set up in the charge of Mrs McIntyre and her band of helpers, including some mothers, who cooked 200 meals a day in a kitchen designed for 50. The Latymer Boat Club was re-established using the boat house and boats belonging to Eton College while football, cricket and other team games were played on as many as 12 different grounds in Slough. Every attempt was made to create a settled routine given the general uncertainty and inflexibility over billetting.

During the war many schools evacuated from London were so widely dispersed over the English countryside that their own character and individuality vanished and they reached near-collapse. It was the great achievement of Fred Wilkinson and his staff that this never happened to Latymer. By the end of 1939 they had succeeded in bringing together the whole school on one site on a daily basis. Although numbers were down from the total of 816 boys who had been on the roll at the beginning of the summer term, the unity of the school during the difficult days of the early part of the war was its strength and held it together when many others were falling apart.

Nevertheless it was not easy. The unsettling effect of the changes wrought by the war affected all schoolchildren. School inspectors reported at the end of the war that the educational progress of the average child had been retarded by as much as a year and that "there was evidence of unsettlement and lack of interest

Latymer Upper boys at Eton College boat house, 1941, where the Latymer Boat Club was re-established during the war.

in the more arduous aspects of school work". It took time for the boys to settle down in Slough. Their attitude towards the town was not helped by rumours that "Slough and its factory chimneys resembled a well-filled pin-cushion". Many boys never really warmed to Slough as a place, a feeling not helped by "the gaunt building at Slough, with the peeling green distempered walls and dark, mine-like corridors", and this tended to promote an apathy among them which had never been experienced at Hammersmith. In July 1942 *The Latymerian* reported that "It was almost too late when we realised exactly how many of our pre-war standards had been swirled away with the torrent of war. Those standards are now being regained but it will require continual effort to advance against the torrent". This was made more difficult by a relaxation in admission standards during the war which saw some boys enter the school who would not normally have been allowed to do so. The headmaster noted that it was the senior boys who were most disturbed by the war itself. The idea that their call-up papers could arrive at any moment saw the gradual evolution of their intellectual development replaced by hurry and scurry, with boys trying to do too much too quickly too young. At Slough the conversation was of planes and tanks, not yachts on the pond or kites in the park. With billets scattered within a 50-mile radius of Slough, the lengthy daily journeys to school took their toll. Many boys, as the war continued, returned home, travelling daily from London to Slough. The head pointed to the remarkable achievements recorded by some of them in the most difficult of circumstances, such as the boy cycling daily from Guildford who won a Cambridge scholarship and another who cycled 4,000 miles in a year to school and gained eight distinctions at school certificate. But the work of many more must have been badly affected by long journeys every day to school, sometimes, at the height of the bombing, after night after sleepless night spent in shelters. Once they reached school, there was a non-stop school timetable in operation (from 9.25 am to 3.10 pm in winter, to cater for train times and an earlier black-out, and from 9.25 am until 3.40 pm in summer), and terms were extended to make up for the teaching time that was lost. Boys also had to contend with a constant state of flux among the staff. Between September 1939 and Easter 1942, for instance, the school lost 13 members of staff. Younger teachers, like Wilf Sharp and George Offiler, were called up. Miss Parry-Okeden was joined by several other temporary female teachers who often had a rough time at the hands of the boys. Mrs Wiggans, however, at least had the advantage of having Mr Wiggans to support her. Some masters, like "Beaky" Palmer and Fred Weekes, came out of retirement. Often groups of boys were allocated to take over responsibility for school duties previously undertaken by staff who had now left. Yet, despite these difficulties, which often led to the school being short of a full complement of staff, a timetable was maintained which was virtually identical to peace-time. Extra-curricular activities, however, were difficult to sustain for many of the same reasons: long journeys between home or billet and school, the necessity to leave school promptly to catch trains, and a reduction in experienced staff. The scouts lost their scoutmaster, the boat club lost its coach. Home football matches were played on grounds as far apart as Slough, Whitton Park, and Wormwood Scrubs, and even further distances had to be travelled to away matches. Team games became increasingly difficult to organise and gave way to a greater emphasis upon athletics and gymnastics. One old boy later wrote bitterly about the cross-country runs he had to endure in winter: "What miserable days they were as we ran over the fields and the golf course, flooded with winter rain and then frozen. Our shins were cut from the ice we plunged through at every step, though we didn't feel much as our legs were numb from the cold".

The school cadet corps flourished as did the school's own branch of the Air Training Corps. This had been started in 1938 as Air Cadet Squadron No 15 and was the first of its kind to be established at a school, leading to many enquiries from other schools which saw many of them follow Latymer's lead.

By April 1940 350 of the 600 boys attending the school at Slough were living at home. For the 250 who were not, the school premises remained open other than at weekends and Bank Holidays, and special vacation terms were organised for those unable to return home for holidays, which now never exceeded a fortnight. During the summer holidays it became usual for senior boys to attend harvest camps in rural Berkshire and Buckinghamshire. They found it hard work. At the camp at Amersham it was not long before "any idea that the farm labourer's life was an easy one vanished. We learned that the ability to pass examinations does not mean that you can make stooks that will keep standing when the wind blows, or build a really stable haystack. We learned, in short, that the black-coated city worker is not quite so clever as he thinks". The boys worked hard, ate heartily and slept well. They made such a good impression with the farmers and, despite bruises and blisters, enjoyed themselves so much that they were happy to accept invitations to the same farms in subsequent years.

However well the school had been organised at Slough, the governors were always looking to reopen the school at Hammersmith where it really belonged. After the boys had been evacuated, parts of the empty buildings had been used to house a variety of voluntary organisations, such as the WVS, and several rooms, including the gymnasium, had been taken over for the storage of 500 tons of flour. The first opportunity to reopen the school at Hammersmith came in early 1940 when the LCC was reopening schools as emergency secondary

Latymer Upper was the first school to form an air defence cadet squadron in Britain, in 1941.

Speech day, 1944 at the school. Mayor Alderman E E Woods (centre) with the mayors of Kensington and Chelsea, the headmaster and Sir Marshall Hays.

Bomb damage to the school on 12 October 1940 at 7.40pm. Apart from the gym, which was destroyed, damage was minimal.

schools. Since these emergency schools would not retain their original identity, however, the governors decided against the idea. In the summer of 1940, however, the LCC told the governors that the Latymer Upper School could be re-opened at Hammersmith for classes of boys up to the age of 14. On 9 September 1940 212 boys returned to school at Hammersmith.

The decision to re-establish the lower half of the school at Hammersmith was important in preparing roots for the time when the whole school would be reunited in London but in practical terms it made a great deal of extra work for the staff, some of whom taught at Hammersmith in the morning and at Slough in the afternoon. Two speech days were held at two locations on the same day with the chairman of governors, Sir Marshall Hays, and the headmaster travelling as rapidly as possible between the two. School life at Hammersmith was also frequently interrupted by air raids. (Dr Hartog, the French master, was doing the "*Comment s'appelle-t-il?*" routine when the sound of a German bomber was heard overhead. "*Comment s'appelle-t-il?*" was the question. As one the class responded amid laughter "*Il s'appelle Jerry!*") The only serious damage the school suffered from bombs came during October 1940 when an oil bomb destroyed the gymnasium, manual training room and the flour stored there. Otherwise any other damage to the roofs, doors and windows was superficial. But there were some close misses. Across the road, on the far side of Ravenscourt Station, the Flora Gardens school was completely destroyed. A man was killed and the front wall of the school damaged by a bomb falling opposite the school. The school caretaker, Mr Crawley, worked all hours during the war to ensure that the school was always clean, no matter how much dust had been dislodged by bomb blasts. Underground shelters were eventually prepared in the basement of the New Buildings which enabled work to be continued during raids. One boy vividly remembers being shown a film in the basement which had been obtained by the

Sir Marshall Hays JP, Chairman of the Board of Governors during the War.

Awarded the D.F.C.—Our picture is of Sqdn.-Ldr. Ro... Turton ...omas

Beat Off 15 Planes, Saved Convoy

"HE has always told me that being a fighter-pilot is a fine holiday," declared Mrs. Ethel Burr, of High Road, Chiswick, when a News Chronicle reporter told her last night that her son, Flying-Officer Arthur Henry Burr (22) had been awarded the D.F.C. for beating off single-handed 15 enemy aircraft.

"In September," says the official citation, "15 enemy aircraft attempted an attack on a convoy in the Arctic Ocean. Flying-Officer Burr, whose aircraft was launched from catapult from the deck of one of the ships . . . destroyed one of the attackers and drove the others off.

"After ensuring that the enemy had abandoned their at-

Press cuttings regarding the exploits of three of the many of the school's Second World War heroes.

head on a visit he had made to the Soviet Union. It was the tale of Gulliver's Travels retold as a piece of Communist propaganda, an instructive exercise for the boys in the evils of propaganda. The disruption to lessons was particularly acute later in the war when V-bombs were falling over London. During the summer of 1944 boys sitting their School Certificate examinations endured a continuous air attack on the capital. Sadly two boys who sat and passed those examinations did not live to receive their certificates. Air raids became such an accepted part of daily routine at this time that 90 boys taking gym in the hall never batted an eyelid when a V1 flying bomb or doodlebug was heard overhead. Boys playing football at Wood Lane (where allotments had once again been prepared as part of the Dig For Victory campaign and which had been used for mooring barrage balloons) barely interrupted the match as doodlebugs flew over them. When a V2 rocket came down with a blast close by the school during morning assembly, there was no panic as prayers and hymns continued without a pause. Such elan made quite an impression upon a visiting American headmaster.

By Easter 1942 there were some 300 boys at Hammersmith, under the direction of Mr Stollery, known from his cherubic complexion as "Cupid", and the headmaster could tell the governors that "this part of the school is now established in its own right". With its own sports teams and other activities all the school facilities were in use. A fencing club was started and swimming and rowing were revived. The Junior Gild was enthusiastically revived (it had lain dormant at Slough) and "promises soon to regain its full and ancient glory". Hammersmith conducted its own "experiment in democracy", very much in tune with the changing times. From September 1941 the highest form in the school, the Lower Vths, met monthly to discuss how best to organise life in the school. *The Latymerian* reported at the end of 1941 that "We doubt if ever there has been such an enthusiastic lower school as there is now".

The numbers at Hammersmith grew steadily. In the Christmas term of 1942, the school roll rose to 780, including, remarkably, 219 new boys. Of these 246 were still at Slough and 534 were at Hammersmith. One year later, on 9 September 1943, Latymer Upper returned at last to Hammersmith, leaving behind at Slough only 58 boys whose parents did not wish to have them back in London. 793 boys attended the school that day. The surroundings were alien for many of them but there was no friction as the two halves of the school finally came together again. The Latymer tradition of tolerance and broadmindedness had survived.

Reunited, there was an upsurge of enthusiasm. Dormant societies and activities were revived, like the physical society, the boxing club and the round-the-river race, while new ones were started, such as the music club. Under the direction of a new arrival to the teaching staff, G G Sexty, the first school concert since the outbreak of war was held in April 1944. The orchestra played, although it was without cellos and basses, there was choral singing from the revived school choir and the newly formed first and second form choirs, and there were instrumental pieces. The choir performed the *Messiah* at Christmas 1944 and was involved in the daily services. The new open spirit of the times saw an upsurge in visits to lectures, plays and exhibitions by senior boys. It seemed as if the school had never moved away and boded well for the post-war future of the school which the headmaster and the governors had already begun to consider.

At Remembrance Day in November 1944, when the roll call of the school's dead from two wars were solemnly read out, the school vice-captain wrote "Yes, the heroes of the Great War are remembered each year. So now are others ... young men who still live in our memories. Youths who, a few months ago, were among us, laughing and working with us, sharing our lives". Such lives included several brothers, like Ralph and Ivan Burger and P J and A C Shearman, and two recent school captains, M Brandreth from 1935 to 1936 who died in 1941 and C L Fox, school captain in 1940 and one of the greatest schoolboy sprinters produced by the school, who was killed in 1944. Mr Wilkinson was so moved by Fox's death that he found himself unable to continue with assembly after he had made the announcement. Tommy Waddams, however, now second master and standing below the stage, refused to let the headmaster walk off and made him go back. The names of 119 Old Latymerians who had given their lives during the 1939–1945 conflict were added to those who had died during the previous war. A memorial window was unveiled in their honour on Founder's Day 1949. The headmaster concluded his eloquent address by saying

there is nothing which we shall do for the rest of our days which is not vouchsafed to us by their sacrifice. They struggled to give us peace; to ensure freedom and happiness; to reinstate justice as the sovereign law; to bring back decency, tolerance and kindliness into our habitual ways of life; to remind a world riddled with hate and spite of "England's old good manners, its old good humour and its old good nature".

Therefore no memorial to them can have any meaning, no grief for them any sincerity, no thought of reunion any reality, unless each of us separately and all of us collectively as a society are determined that the ideals for which they fought shall be by us firmly and finally established.

Central lights from the Second World War memorial window in the Great Hall.

91

CHAPTER SEVEN

'In Good Heart and Shape'

REVIVAL AND CONSOLIDATION

1945–1971

During the 1930s even conservative educational opinion had come to accept secondary education should be open to all those talented enough to benefit, regardless of class. Here were the first inklings of a movement towards free secondary education for all which was accelerated by the changing attitudes created by the war. In the early 1940s there was general agreement that education should be separated into three progressive stages, primary, secondary and further education, that all secondary fees should be abolished, and that parity should be achieved in all types of secondary school. Wilkinson was one of four London secondary school headmasters who published their own scheme in 1942 for post-war educational reconstruction. This proposed that all schools not currently under state control should be brought within the remit of the Ministry of Education or abolished. New community schools for 11–16 and 11–18 were advocated, providing an education for every child "on a footing of equality". After the age of 13, children would spend half their time on citizenship-related studies and the other half on developing their own aptitudes. University selection would be conducted through selection boards and maintenance grants would be introduced. The plan was described as "uncompromisingly democratic" but that was the spirit of the age. During the consultations which were undertaken before the passage of the 1944 Education Act, Wilkinson was determined to ensure that aided schools were neither abolished nor absorbed within the direct control of the local education authorities. The chairman of governors, Sir Marshall Hays, was able to make detailed comment both upon the Bill and upon the LCC's plans for the reorganisation of secondary education through the newly established Association of Governing Bodies of London Aided Secondary Schools. The Act raised the school-leaving age to 15 (achieved in 1947) and then to 16 (which had to wait until 1970). It divided secondary education into three types – grammar, technical and modern – and it was to be provided free, without any means testing or other restrictions. The drawback of the Act, in the words of A J P Taylor, was that it "unwittingly created a new class division between those who were clever enough to get into a grammar school at 'eleven plus' and those who were not".

Opposite page: Rivercourt House, which is now the Latymer Upper prep school, in about 1900.

The passage of the Act brought the Latymer Foundation to an educational cross-roads. There was not only the future of the Latymer Upper School to consider but also that of the Latymer Foundation School. Both schools had to select one of four options under the Act: independence, voluntary-aided status, direct grant status or maintained status. As far as the Foundation School was concerned, the governors wanted to see it remain within the purview of the Foundation. Once again there was discussion about the possibility of reorganising the Foundation School to become the junior department of the Upper School. Given the plans the governors had for the Upper School, the burden of carrying the costs of a reorganised Foundation School was one they could not afford at the time. For the same reason, they rejected voluntary-aided status which carried with it certain financial responsibilities the Foundation was reluctant to meet. These largely related to the Foundation's share of any costs involved in the rebuilding of the school, which would be a necessity in the near future because the old premises were now thoroughly inadequate. Because of the close links the school had developed with the LCC, approval of an application for direct grant status was unlikely. Maintained status would place it entirely under the control of the LCC and the governors were not prepared to countenance that option. In fact the governors agreed that the school should be closed rather than lose its identity. At this point the London Diocesan Board of Education stepped in and offered to fund the building costs that the Foundation would have incurred. With this support, the governors agreed that the Foundation School should opt for voluntary-aided status.

For one reason or another, the rebuilding of the Foundation School as a secondary modern school for 300 pupils was not planned to take place until 1961–1962. By then, however, the LCC had revised its own plans and, with the support of the London Diocesan Board, intended to merge the Foundation School, which was now considered to be too small, with two other existing secondary schools on a site in Fulham. This was strongly opposed by the Foundation and the governors repeated their view that the school should be closed if it lost its identity. The possibility of the Foundation School surviving in its own right either as a secondary school or as a primary school were both considered and both rejected as impractical. The decision that the school should be closed, in July 1963, was reaffirmed. This provoked a concerted campaign by pupils, parents and staff to reverse the decision during which the Foundation governors found it necessary to point out that the decision had been forced upon them by the change in the LCC's educational policies. Moreover, the governors "felt that there could be no justification for diverting Foundation funds to the use of a school divorced from the Foundation". The decision stood, the school was closed, and the site was sold for the benefit of Foundation funds. This was a sad end for a school which could trace its origins back 236 years to those first eight poor almsboys sent to Fulham for their education. There was a special assembly for the last Foundation School boys held in the hall of Latymer Upper in July 1963. The Foundation School's war memorial book was handed over to the Upper School for safekeeping. Upon the demolition of the Foundation School some years later, the foundation stone from the opening of the buildings in 1863 was saved and incorporated within the entrance of the swimming pool

William Wheatley teaching chemistry in 1951. He was the author of The History of Edward Latymer and his Foundations *and other books.*

being built at the same time at the Upper School, a lasting reminder of the close association which had always existed between the two.

As far as the future of the Latymer Upper School was concerned after the 1944 Education Act, the governors were faced with similar choices. The LCC was pressing the school to choose voluntary-aided status. The school would continue to receive a maintenance grant from the council. No fees would be charged but the LCC would make up any loss incurred without call on the income of the Foundation, which would continue to be spent at the discretion of the governors. This all sounded fine but there was no doubt that the financial influence of the council over the school would increase under this arrangement. The governors were also concerned at the much larger role the council would assume in the selection of pupils. In voluntary-aided schools where fees were abolished the LCC would be in charge of selection. Parental preference would determine the choice of school and only where demand exceeded supply would the school have the right to select pupils. The council was also hinting that it wanted to reduce the numbers of out-of-county pupils attending its schools. This was of particular concern to the governors at Latymer Upper which, as far as the place of pupils' residence was concerned, was the most non-local of all London's voluntary-aided schools (in 1945 57% of pupils lived out-of-county and only 16% came from Hammersmith). It seemed obvious that the nature of the school would inevitably change if it was decided to adopt voluntary-aided status.

For a similar reason little consideration was given to seeking complete independence. While it was likely that the local education authorities would continue to send scholars to the school, there was no certainty that this would be so. Fees would have to rise considerably if the school became independent and this would inevitably alter the nature of the fee-paying intake. After careful consideration, the governors decided that the best route to secure relative independence and maintain the nature of the school would be to apply for recognition as a direct grant grammar school to the Ministry of Education. In return for annual capitation grants received directly from the Ministry, the school would have to offer 25% of its places free each year to primary school pupils while the local education authorities could request an allocation each year from the school of a further 25% of places, known as reserved places. The remaining places, known as residuary places, were open to fee-payers who, depending upon their income, were eligible for reduced fees, the difference being paid directly to the school by the Ministry. Overall control of the school and its finances remained with the Ministry, but the governors retained a fair degree of independence and were no longer beholden to the LCC. Staff, pupils and old boys were all supportive of the governors' decision and, despite the opposition of the LCC, the governors had an ally in the Middlesex County Council, where half of the school's pupils came from.

The Ministry approved the school's application in the summer of 1945. The school had no difficulty in fulfilling the main criteria for approval, that it had a substantial endowed income from which capital projects would have to be funded (it was one of the most well-endowed aided schools in London); and that a large number of its pupils went on to university (its record spoke for itself). *The Latymerian* wrote that the school would now be "free from arbitrary interference" and that "our system of admission ... will remain based strictly on a boy's intrinsic merit and not on the financial capacity of his parents".

Boys at the school during and after the war remarked how seamlessly the transition from war to peace was made. Considering the disadvantages the school laboured under immediately after the war, this was quite an achievement. When the few stragglers still at Slough came back for the beginning of the autumn term of 1945, there were 860 boys at the school, 104 of whom were in the sixth form. This was a record number but the headmaster, partly to relieve the general shortage of secondary school places at the time, was known to have his sights on 1,000. But the school was already excessively over-crowded and displaying the signs of wear and tear caused by the war and the lack of investment in the school during that period. The aged school heating system struggled on but the winter weather of 1946–1947 completely defeated it for a whole week. Boys sat in class wrapped in overcoats and mufflers, clutching candles and torches carried from room to room to provide light and a little heat. There were several classrooms which were so swept with draughts that the temperature never got above freezing, even when the heating system was working. Remarkably, despite the appalling conditions, Mrs Crawley and her staff still produced 500 school lunches without any light and with most of the kitchen equipment out of action. Eventually a rota system had to be imposed because the dining room and kitchens were simply inadequate for the 650 boys taking lunch but this resulted in each boy missing three out of ten lunches. Because the school was still without a gymnasium, gym was taken by Mr Wiggans in the school hall in primitive conditions and at an obvious disadvantage to those boys being taught in the classrooms which surrounded it, as Mr Wiggans' loud voice boomed out and reverberated around the rafters. Boys were still using "tattered text books long since worn out". The common room was several members short and staff were over-

F G Gregory, second master, who taught modern languages at the school from 1931–68. He organised the school's first trip to Switzerland, in 1947.

stretched. Class sizes which should have been no greater than 30 still varied from 31 to 36 at the end of 1949. The allotments at Wood Lane had produced a recurrence of the playing field's drainage problems. It now turned into a quagmire so easily that often games could not take place. It was hardly surprising under these sort of burdens that one master joining the staff in 1949 should later comment that "the effects of the war were still visible on both staff and boys".

Harmony during this difficult period, "a dismal cloud of control and shortage", was obviously helped by the fact that the school had returned almost in its entirety to Hammersmith two years' previously in 1943. The school routine which had been established then held good now, with the advantage of being uninterrupted by bombs and rockets. Then there was that tolerance that came from the classlessness that was perhaps the school's greatest strength, born of mixing boys from the poorest parts of Fulham and the most prosperous parts of Harrow, and the friendly but disciplined atmosphere within the school created not only by the boys but as much by the example of the staff and the headmaster. The hardships of war too had created boys who were tougher and more resilient, capable of taking peacetime difficulties in their stride.

Mr Wilkinson, having kept the school intact during the war and led it from being an LCC voluntary-aided school to direct grant status, wanted to continue in 1945 where he had left off in 1939 and carry on with the development of a more open, more broadly based school. This did not mean that he wanted to forget about the war which had just ended. On the contrary, the Second World War emphatically reaffirmed his belief in the need to avoid war and in the importance of international understanding without regard for class or race. In essence this was no more than a logical extension of the ethos which had long been traditional at Latymer Upper and was in fact something being considered by a number of schools around the country. As had happened after the end of the First World War, the role of the corps was diminished "as the school once again assumes its true role as an institution which places the ideals of scholarly culture above those of efficient regimentation and destruction". The flags of all nations were hung around the hall. Boys from abroad were welcomed into the school as pupils (at one time in one of the third forms there were boys from Nepal, Burma, Pakistan and India). Boys took part in the Council for Education in World Citizenship which led to the formation at the school of the International Society. A branch of the Commonwealth Society was also started at the school. On one occasion to further the spirit of internationalism, the headmaster announced at assembly one morning that special leave of absence would be granted to any boy from the sixth form who would travel abroad and finance his trip from work found in the country in which he was staying. Two boys went to work on Norwegian farms, another went to Stockholm, one went to Rome and several more travelled to the south of France. Foreign travel began again in the summer of 1947 when a party of 88 boys with Mr Gregory visited Switzerland. It was a sad revival since one of the boys, Colin Wright, a school prefect and the captain of cricket, died from heart failure while bathing. This did not deter further visits to Switzerland, Austria, France and Yugoslavia during the summer holidays while the school's first winter tour took place in Austria during the Christmas break of 1950.

Mayor W H Brind talking to Major T C Stewart MC after the Cadets' Inspection, Wood Lane, 1952.

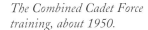

The Combined Cadet Force training, about 1950.

Above: *The mayor of Hammersmith at an exhibition of paintings by Latymer boys and German boys from the Gelehrtenschule des Johanneum, Hamburg.* Below: *Headmaster Wilkinson at the Johanneum.*

„Persons matter much more than politics" war die persön-iche Überzeugung von Frederick Wilkinson, der 1947 als Headmaster der Latymer Upper School die ersten Kontakte zum Johanneum aufnahm. Schon 1954 konnte Mr. Wilkin-on vor dem NWDR-Mikrophon von einem Erfolg der Partnerschaft sprechen

Opposite: *"The school is so very much more than an examination machine"*: From top: *Sack race, 1950s; School scouts at camp, Sevenoaks, 1952; School play* The Rhesus of Euripides, *1952; Wilkinson rehearsing for a MAD evening, 1950s.*

But Wilkinson's greatest and longest-standing achievement in this sphere at Latymer came through the school-twinning arrangements he began with schools from Germany and France. He fervently believed that "Somehow we have got to enlarge our patriotism so that we may feel the same degree of loyalty to Europe as we do to our own country", that "European union will be still-born until it has become the natural and passionate practice of the common man to make his friendships wherever he likes".

It was entirely the headmaster's idea that links should be forged in 1947 with a Hamburg school founded in 1529, the Gelehrtenschule des Johanneum, a venture which he described as "an experiment in friendship". The pattern for this experiment was, of course, the relationship which had been built up between his previous school and a school in Berlin during the late 1920s and 1930s (and which was resurrected after the war). The Johanneum Society was started at Latymer Upper on 13 October 1947. It was a humane and far-sighted gesture which inevitably brought some criticism but also generated much support. Nearly 60 boys from the Lower Vths upwards participated in exchanging letters with their German contemporaries and parcels of books and food were sent over from the school to Hamburg. On 2 December that year Günther von Allwörden wrote to the school from the Johanneum accepting the headmaster's invitation "to enter into co-operation and comradeship". These links have remained intact ever since. The first exchange visit took place in July 1948 when the Foreign Office was persuaded to allow a party of five boys and one master from Hamburg to visit Latymer Upper for three weeks. On Remembrance Day in the following year Latymer boys were joined by several German boys in calling the names of the school's war dead. When a party of boys from Latymer visited the Johanneum for the first time in the summer of 1949, the uneasiness they felt at visiting the land of a former enemy was overcome not only by the impact of the enormous wartime devastation they witnessed in Hamburg but also by the genuinely sincere welcome they received from their hosts. Their headmaster hoped that such visits, which have taken place ever since, would demonstrate that "although our differences may be considerable, what we have in common is more considerable still".

The success of the German venture inspired several further attempts to develop similar links with schools in other European countries. In the early 1950s Latymer Upper established relationships with schools in Stockholm and Oslo but these were short-lived. At Easter 1955 28 boys travelled to Paris to begin a new scheme of association with the Lycée Chaptal. This lasted until 1961, falling victim of the dread so many schoolboys have of venturing on individual exchange visits and ending up with people they find it impossible to get on with. In 1963, however, another French school was contacted and an exchange scheme has been maintained between one French school or another to this day.

Wilkinson pressed on with extending extra-curricular activities in other directions. He would write in later years that "The school is so very much more than an examination machine. It abounds in activity and I like to think that we have managed so to integrate our lives that everything we undertake not only has scholarly quality but intellectual, physical and spiritual harmony as well". There were many more visits to places of interest as well as to theatres and concert halls. Play readings provided the first opportunity in 1946 to invite girls from the Godolphin and Latymer School, the Foundation's sister school across the road, to join the Latymer boys. In the following year boys were permitted to attend the dance organised by the Old Latymerians at Hammersmith Town Hall although it was reported that "Many of the fairer sex will testify that Latymerians, past and present, are greater experts on the football field than on the dance floor". The first dance at the school took place in the school hall in 1946 under the auspices of the boat club. It was not until 1954 that the first school dance proper was held in Hammersmith Town Hall, when invitations were sent to girls from a number of neighbouring schools. New societies were founded including the Philosophical Society, the eagerness of whose members saw meetings last until all hours on a Friday evening. Debating returned in the guise of the Freston Society, created in 1950 and taking its name from the Suffolk village connected with the Latymer family.

Perhaps the most enlivening of all the activities particularly fostered by the headmaster were drama and music. In May 1948 the annual Musical and Dramatic Evenings began. (They quickly became known by their acronym as MAD evenings although it took the head some time before he woke up to the consequences of setting the boys so easy a target.) The play which usually formed a part of each evening was put on with only a week's rehearsal, made possible only because the tradition of the Gild enabled boys to acquire an acting technique which became second nature. The plays were always personally directed by Mr Wilkinson, who effectively ran the school for that week from the Hammersmith Town Hall, where the evenings were held. He liked nothing more than to muster a huge cast of boys in an action-packed play but his demands upon other members of his staff, who were responsible for rapidly putting together staging, sets, and lighting, severely tested their patience at times. MAD evenings were an annual event although from 1954 onwards they alternated every third year with the Triennial School Exhibition, a display of craft work and art which Wilkinson had originally devised to fill a gap in the summer term for boys who had completed their examinations (the Exhibitions eventually came to an end when examining boards were changed). Since drama found an outlet in the MAD evenings as well as in the activities of the Gild, it was often difficult to find the time for the production of plays on their own but they did occur and were beginning to find a regular place in the school calendar by the time Wilkinson retired in 1957. As far as music was concerned, first under G G Sexty until 1947 and then Clifford Harman, it received an impetus it had never before had at Latymer Upper. For a brief period in the early 1950s, Clifford Harman's assistant was John Poole, who later went on to conduct the BBC Singers. The choir sang in Bach's "St Matthew Passion" in the autumn of 1945, and the school orchestra was resurrected under Kenneth Popplewell, an Old Latymerian who had a distinguished career as an orchestral violinist with the Royal Philharmonic and BBC Symphony Orchestras. In 1954 the school orchestra, already renowned for its *esprit de corps* in the traditional Latymerian manner, became a full orchestra, with strings, woodwind, brass and tympani, and all except one of its members (a professional trumpeter) were Latymerians. Choir, orchestra and band often featured in the annual MAD evenings. Joint activities with the girls of the Godolphin and Latymer School were extended to

A race at Wood Lane in the early 1950s.

A novel method of hurdling, 1950s.

music in 1956 when a joint choir made an anonymous radio broadcast for the BBC from the school hall.

Other clubs and societies were revived, such as the swimming club, chess club and field club. The scouts continued to thrive and the school was selected in 1957 to take part in the pilot scheme for the Duke of Edinburgh's Award Scheme. The Gild was restored to its central position in school activities. Those boys who had kept the tradition alive during the war when the Gild existed only in its junior form were now enthusiastic participants in the senior Gild. The annual Jantaculum once again became an event of which it was said that "the pleasure of watching is nothing to the pleasure of playing". Through the Gild the school performed for only the second time in its history a Shakespeare play, *Julius Caesar*, in the spring of 1951. Michael Redgrave was the Gild's guest in 1953 and, in writing to convey his thanks for the enjoyable time he had spent in the school, remarked that he had found "the atmosphere of the place wonderfully warm and alive in the way that one would like all schools to be". It was not only Latymer boys who recognised that there was something special about the atmosphere of the place. The Junior Gild was renamed the Middle School Society when it was re-established in 1946 but eventually became The Journeymen in 1953. The Apprentices was reborn in 1950 and three years later a similar society, the Rivercourt Society, was created for boys in the preparatory department.

The general impression was that Wilkinson was not really interested in sport. His record at university and at Wallasey Grammar School, as well as his initiative in establishing the school boat club, showed this to be false. The truth was perhaps that his love for drama in particular outshone any interest he had in sport. Nevertheless that interest was there and showed itself after the war. Boys from the period recall especially the late 1940s as a golden period in Latymer sporting history with strong teams in football, cricket, rowing and athletics. In 1946 the school's six football teams lost only two matches between them. In the same year came Latymer's first real success in rowing when a strong 1st VIII won the Pennant in the Lightweight Class in the Head of the River Race, beating all other schools taking part, the Junior Challenge Cup at the Chiswick Regatta, their first victory in a status event, and also the Open VIII at the Hammersmith Regatta. Nevertheless, it was only in 1956, after 18 years of using borrowed,

100

patched-up and second-hand boats, that the boat club launched its first new boat, which was appropriately named "Wilkie". Before that, for many years during the Christmas holidays, Alan Watson and a band of boys would haul the best boat in through a classroom window and into the long school corridor, uninterrupted in those days by fire doors, and strip, revarnish and repair it.

It was under Mr Wilkinson that rugby had been introduced at Wallasey Grammar School. There had been a strong rugby lobby at Latymer Upper for some time and the school rugby football club was started in January 1949 under Mr Dudley. The first match was played against an ex-servicemen's XV from St Mary's Teacher Training College in March. It was not surprising that the school lost 28–0. Cricket flourished and the school for the first time employed a cricket coach when Jack Hearne, of Middlesex and England, joined the staff in 1951. Tennis was revived and three hard courts were built in 1954, the same year in which a new gymnasium was erected to replace the one destroyed in the war. It had taken until 1952 before the necessary building licence for a new gymnasium had been obtained because of continuing government controls. In 1955 the school celebrated its Jubilee Games Year with some notable sporting achievements. The school soccer team won 13 of its 15 fixtures, recording 75 goals for and only 27 against, although the two matches lost ended an unbroken record of wins stretching back over three years. For the fourth year in a row the senior swimming team became the Senior Team Champions of London Grammar Schools. The senior athletics team went unbeaten in all school matches. By now all boys had the opportunity of playing 12 different sports (football, cricket, rowing, rugby, tennis, squash, badminton, swimming, water polo, athletics, cross-country and baseball). The house system was still in use for sporting competitions but enthusiasm for it had waned dramatically since the war and the system was almost defunct by the time of Wilkinson's retirement in 1957, finally being abolished two years later.

If the boys were being given greater opportunities to expand their horizons both in terms of what they did at school and in relation to the world outside school, then Wilkinson was also keen to see parents develop more of an interest

Above: *Jack Hearne, cricket coach, coaching at Wood Lane in 1952.*
Below: *The rugby club beating Hampton Grammar School, 1952.*

Rowing on the Thames, going past the Harrods depository, 1950s.

Morning assembly, 1950s.

in their sons' school. A parents' society would have been started at the school but for the intervention of the war. At the end of 1945 the Parents' Gild finally got off the ground and ten meetings were held in the first term of its existence. It was a great success and well supported both by parents and by staff. Topics discussed at meetings between parents and staff included the difficulties of boys in the C and D forms, homework, school meals, the admission of younger boys, options for the Lower Vths, and admission to university.

What, of course, continued to concern parents most was the quality of the teaching their sons received and the academic standards within the school. The curriculum, in line with Wilkinson's policies elsewhere in the school, was broadened in several respects, including the introduction of economics and Russian to the timetable. The older staff who had served the school so well during the war made way at last for younger staff, not only those returning from war service but also new appointments. 26 of the 44 full-time members of staff at the school in 1953 had been appointed since 1945. There were years when the school had mixed academic results, notably at school certificate level in 1947 and at university scholarship level in 1951 (when only two awards were obtained, the lowest number since 1916). On the other hand, in the first year of the new General Certificates of Education in 1951, 108 out of 118 boys passed O level and 61 out of 63 passed A level, and in 1952 the school recorded 16 university scholarship winners. It was this latter pattern which remained the standard at Latymer Upper. Wilkinson never really liked GCEs, which permitted candidates to obtain certificates in single subjects unlike the School Certificate, which could only be obtained if candidates gained a pass a minimum of six subjects, including English, maths, science and modern languages. GCEs he regarded as "one supreme level of total mediocrity". This remark was perhaps indicative of the degree of emphasis still placed upon academic achievement at the school and which led to the adoption of a five-year GCE course at the school, with each boy taking a minimum of five and a maximum of eight GCEs. This was criticised by inspectors in 1953 for its "limited objective of success" which, as a result, encouraged boys to choose too many subjects, held back abler boys from an earlier start on advanced work, and left others deeply frustrated when, after spending five years compelled to study a subject, they had still not reached examination standard. The inspectors recommended a rationalisation of the course in the fourth year and an increase in the number of options available for boys. The inspectors also found that there was still a tendency within the school to underrate the ability of C, D and E formers, commenting that "the great majority of them have considerable capacity and they would almost certainly achieve more if more were expected of them".

The results which confirmed Latymer Upper's place as a school of high academic achievement were won despite the fact that many of the difficulties faced by the school in 1945 still existed well into the 1950s. The school's examination results and the opportunities it offered boys in other fields consolidated its popularity. Places were always heavily over-subscribed in spite of the constantly increasing school roll. Part of the reason for rising numbers was the implementation of Wilkinson's pre-war plan to create a separate preparatory department. In 1951 the governors purchased Rivercourt House, a fine early nineteenth century

house on the banks of the river, which had first been offered to them in the 1920s. This housed not only a preparatory department of some 50 boys aged between 9 and 10 in the charge of Mrs Wiggans but also provided space on the first and second floors for the burgeoning sixth form (141 members in 1953). By 1955 there were 1,039 boys in the school. Overcrowding was more acute than ever but government controls over building, which were not abolished until that year, meant that it had been very difficult to obtain the necessary building licences to provide the additional accommodation necessary. A new kitchen and dining room were provided in 1947, and the new gymnasium was built in 1954, but otherwise that was all until 1955. Instead the governors had instructed the headmaster on several occasions to see that overcrowding got no worse by restricting admissions but Wilkinson never paid more than lip service to these edicts. It was hardly surprising that the school inspectors in 1953 should criticise class sizes which now varied between 35 and 37 or accommodation which was often inadequate. They had pointed out that too many boys were being taught in too little accommodation by too few staff. The existing staff, for whom the inspectors had a high regard, had insufficient free periods and were often overstretched. Some additional appointments were made as a result but there were at least two subsequent cases of members of staff breaking down entirely because of overwork. The chemistry laboratory was old-fashioned, the art room, woodwork shop and staff room were too small, the library was "unlikely to attract any but the most determined readers". So many of these criticisms could have come straight from the inspectors' report of 1933. As a result of this report an extensive series of room changes was implemented to try and rectify the faults identified by the inspectors. There were plans for a new chemistry laboratory above the old dining room, a new physics laboratory and lecture room, and a larger hall and kitchen/dining room. A new biology department was being built

Top left: *Rivercourt House, Upper Mall, about 1900, offered to Latymer in the 1920s and bought to house the preparatory department in 1951. Queen Catherine of Braganza* (above), *consort of Charles II, lived in a house on this site 1687–91. It was she who planted the imposing elm trees that lined Upper Mall. The last of these was felled in 1954* (top right).

The new gymnasium as reported in The Latymerian (above), *and* (below) *being opened in 1954 by the chairman of the governors, H H G Bennett.*

above the old one which would then become the history department. Another problem was that the Cromwell Road extension, a scheme which had been talked about since the early 1930s, finally came to fruition in the 1950s and cut the school site in half in 1955. In fact, this latter occurrence turned out to be a blessing disguise. The school received properties in Rivercourt Road in compensation which enabled new building to take place and the school site was transformed from a narrow strip to two rectangles.

The headmaster retired in the summer of 1957. The verdict of the last inspection of the school during his time succinctly summed up his headship: "His patent sincerity of purpose, sensitivity, wide interests and liberal outlook are a very valuable example to the school and his influence with the boys is none the less effective for being unobtrusive". Because of the size of the school he had insisted upon regarding each boy as an individual and avoided regimentation by setting down the minimum of rules and regulations. His personal example was said upon his retirement to have encouraged "the present informal relationship between masters and boys which exists throughout the school". He had widened the opportunities available to boys both inside and outside the classroom. He had kept the school together during the war. He had secured its future through direct grant status (and, in so doing, become the first headmaster of Latymer to be admitted to the Headmasters' Conference). During his final years he had begun the process of improving the school buildings. The school's academic record remained of the highest standards. As a result of Wilkinson's headship, the Latymer Upper School had become a more rounded school. Upon his death after a long retirement in 1978, Wilf Sharp paid him this tribute: "one witnessed the transformation from a Grammar School of high academic reputation and achievement but one at which examination results and University successes were the top priorities to a school where these things still counted for much but became secondary to the building of a school where a boy's individual needs and his relationship with his fellows mattered most".

Building site for the Cromwell Road extension, 1955, which split the school site in half. The subway to connect the two parts is being built in the foreground.

His successor was Kenneth Sutcliffe. His name was only placed on the short-list for interviews after the withdrawal of another candidate but he was the unanimous choice of the governors. Like his two predecessors, Kenneth Sutcliffe was a northerner. He had been educated at Manchester Grammar School before winning a major scholarship to King's College, Cambridge, where he read modern languages. He taught at Stockport Grammar School and the Liverpool Institute before serving during the war as a staff captain with the Intelligence Service at the War Office. In 1946 he was appointed as headmaster of Cockburn High School in Leeds. He was a very different personality to Wilkinson. He was a modest and self-effacing man who preferred to learn about the school from his study rather than from a tour of inspection. He was no less well-informed or approachable but the school was expected to go to him rather than the other way round. He was direct and straightforward with an innate instinct for the heart of the matter, regardless of the waffle he might have to put up with, but he was also affable and possessed a dry sense of humour. He was a man of the utmost integrity, kind and courteous, with a keen understanding of human nature and a humane concern for others. Like Wilkinson, he too shared a concern not only for the brightest and the best but for all the boys as individuals. He was helpful and encouraging towards his staff. He was an authoritative rather than an authoritarian headmaster, a stickler for the maintenance of high standards in every sphere of school life, a tonic for a school which, in the words of one member of staff, had become "a bit slapdash although it was a slapdash school kept in check by Wilkie". Because Kenneth Sutcliffe was such a contrast, the school, both staff and pupils, took some time to accept him. The seal upon his acceptance came at the annual Jantaculum, during the Impossibilities, sketches which made little sense to anyone outside the school, when a boy strode on stage and making a play upon words in a heavy Scottish accent simply said "D'ye no ken? Oh, no, you do!" and made his exit to tumultuous applause.

Kenneth Sutcliffe, Headmaster 1957–71.

One link between the two headmasters was that they both had the same secretary, the remarkable Mrs Hall. The school administration of those days was remarkably compact and for many years Mrs Hall's administrative skills, considerable memory and sharp brain made her an indispensable part of it. She insisted on staying on at the school for the first few years of Kenneth Sutcliffe's term until he was well settled in. Wilkinson had appointed the first school secretary in 1948, when George Terry, an Old Latymerian working for the school's accountants, took on the post until he joined the teaching staff in 1954. By 1960 both the headmaster and the clerk to the governors were complaining about the increasing burden of paperwork, much of which was outside their scope, and Len Woods was appointed the school's first bursar.

The first thing that Kenneth Sutcliffe tackled was the accommodation problem on the school site. He personally undertook a detailed review of the school premises. He considered the biggest disadvantage was that the school was divorced from its playing field. The removal of the school to a new site would have been the ideal solution but he understood the arguments against this. The existing site still possessed certain advantages, in that it was compact and well-located, there were good frontages front and back, and there was still room for expansion. The buildings themselves were excellent in part, notably the hall, the chapel, the recently built gymnasium and some of the classrooms. But the school now catered for more than three times its originally intended capacity. There was an urgent need for more teaching space to remove the need to use unsuitable areas, such as laboratories and lecture rooms, as classrooms and to provide suitable accommodation for the very large sixth form (who numbered 280 at the beginning of the 1959–1960 school year). The only way the whole school could be gathered within the hall was if every boy stood rather than sat so assemblies had to be short (this, however, went down well with staff who remembered the disruption caused to their teaching by Mr Wilkinson's overlong assemblies). In fact, by 1960 the hall was no longer able to cope with the number of boys and daily assemblies were replaced by a weekly assembly. There was a need for a second hall, a better dining room, and a new library. The poor handicraft areas had to be improved, especially since "a rather larger technical element would be advantageous for some of the boys" in a predominantly academic atmosphere.

Larger playing fields, a swimming pool and a boat house would all be desirable. A further report by the headmaster on games facilities in 1961 described them as "extremely inadequate". Because Wood Lane was not large enough for the size of the school, on some afternoons not all boys were able to play games while over-intensive use of a badly drained field rendered it barely playable during winter months. Whitton Park, which was used regularly every Wednesday by the school, was really too far away. The alternatives offered were poor, ranging from swimming which still took place at a public swimming bath to cross-country on "a scarcely varying route". The boat club still had to share the facilities of other clubs. In response to the headmaster's conclusion, which stated that "the school's games arrangements contain too many makeshifts", the governors merely recommended that greater use should be made of Whitton Park, involving hired transport if necessary, and that further drainage work should be carried out at Wood Lane.

As far as funding such major improvements was concerned, the new headmaster realised that the Foundation did not have any large capital sums available. The improvements would have to be financed from revenue and any additions would therefore have to be made piecemeal. Initially the plans prepared as a

The Old Latymerian Association sports pavilion, 1966.

result of this review envisaged the demolition of almost all the buildings on site but, while this option was not ruled out, neither did it gain complete acceptance, and the plan acted more as a guide for the governors than a blueprint. Instead the piecemeal programme of improvements got underway with the building of a new physics laboratory. This extension was completed in the autumn of 1961. With the modernisation of the chemistry laboratories, the school once again had sufficient science accommodation, the previous shortage of which had compelled the introduction of a staggered lunch hour to enable all boys to use the limited facilities. For some time many people, particularly the school rowing coach, Alan Watson, himself an Old Latymerian and an international and Olympic oarsman, had been pressing for a school boathouse. Apart from Eton, Latymer Upper was at the time the only school with a frontage along the Thames. Yet, in contrast to some schools without a school site on the river, such as Westminster and Hampton, Latymer was still without a boathouse of its own. The go-ahead for a building on a site between Rivercourt House and Latymer House was given by the governors in 1960 but had to overcome concern expressed by the Ministry of Education that this project would not prejudice the "urgent necessity" of remodelling the existing school buildings. It was not until 1962 that final plans were approved by the governors and the boathouse was formally opened on 18 March 1964 by the chairman of Henley Royal Regatta, Harold Ricketts. The boathouse provided accommodation for a boatman and Alan Watson was able to recruit the boatman he had known when, as a student at Westminster College, he was a member of the University of London Boat Club. Harry Vincent, an ex-chief petty officer, stayed at Latymer until his retirement in 1989. He terrified novice rowers but was held in nothing but respect and affection by boat club members by the time they left the school. He was also known as a great character along the river.

Harold Rickett, chairman of the Henley Royal Regatta, opening the boathouse, 1963.

Further discussions about building improvements took place between the chairman of governors, Harry Bennett, an Old Latymerian and a director of J Lyons Ltd, the headmaster, Her Majesty's Inspectors and advisers from the Ministry in early 1963. Several main recommendations emerged. One proposed the continued acquisition by the school of properties on the west side of Rivercourt Road which formed the eastern boundary of the school. The school had been buying houses for some years on that side of the road as they came on the market and using them for additional teaching space, and the process was in fact only completed with the purchase of the final vacant property in 1994. Secondly, it was suggested that three of these properties which the school already owned should be demolished and replaced by a sixth form block. Thirdly, a sports hall, swimming pool and new dining hall should be constructed on the southern part of the site on the far side of the Cromwell Road extension while the present gym, which was already too small, should be converted into a new library.

A year later and these plans were no further forward. An editorial in *The Latymerian* at the beginning of 1964 was scathing about the state of the school buildings and commented that "little can be done to the present buildings except, it appears, to raze the whole collection to the ground and start afresh somewhere else which is obviously impracticable". Armed with such ammunition, the head was persistent and told the governors at that time that the choices they faced still

Right: *More building, 1960s. The site of the new dining hall and art department. The site of 20 Rivercourt Road is top right.*
Below: *View of 20 Rivercourt Road by William Bowyer RA. The building is fondly remembered by a generation of Latymer boys.*

Opposite page: *Celebrities at Latymer. From top: Margaret Thatcher, then Secretary of State for Education, arriving to open the new teaching block in 1971; Raphael Wallfisch in his last cello performance as a schoolboy in 1969; Mel Smith and Dr Hilary Jones; Hugh Grant in a school play.*

remained the same – a phased programme of improvements upon the existing site or the wholesale removal of the school to a new site – but a decision could scarcely be put off any longer. As well as a fine academic record, it was important that the school should also offer decent premises and decent playing fields. He suggested that if the governors wished to do so, the time was opportune to investigate the possibility of moving to another site. Most of the school's intake came from Middlesex while fewer and fewer boys came from the immediate neighbourhood. The Foundation had capital funds available to it from the sale of properties in Shepherd's Bush and Hammersmith for the first time and they could be supplemented by the sale of the present site and the Wood Lane playing field. Some time was actually devoted to searching for alternative sites but the board soon gave it up as a hopeless task. (Kenneth Sutcliffe once told his successor that you do not move a school; you close one and open another.) Over the next two years the governors gradually came to the view originally expressed by the headmaster and approved a phased programme of works comprising most of the suggestions made in 1963. Work was expected to begin in 1967 and be completed by the end of 1970. To catch the interest of parents and to raise funds not only for the proposed improvements but also for future additions, the governors also agreed to the head's suggestion that the building programme be linked to the school's first-ever fund-raising appeal.

By the autumn term of 1969, a new block had been built towards the front of the school site which provided physics and biology departments. The old biology laboratory became geography classrooms, the chemistry department was re-equipped and a new school office created. The houses at 16–20 Rivercourt Road which had acted for some years as much needed additional classrooms were demolished and a new teaching block built on the site, which, together with the new dining hall, was opened by the Secretary of State for Education, Margaret Thatcher, in May 1971. The time-scale for all phases of the programme proved impossible to meet but nevertheless significant progress had been made in modernising the school site.

The vigour of the school's corporate life had been one of the things that had impressed Sutcliffe upon his appointment as headmaster. In his quiet way he gave his support to all aspects of this life, leaving them even more vigorous on his departure than he had found them. The MAD evenings could scarcely survive the departure of their founder so were replaced by a competitive Music and Speech Festival. Joint musical events with the Godolphin and Latymer School continued and for a while similar links were developed with Hornsey Girls' School. The standard of music in the school became so good that boys were selected to play in the National Youth Orchestra. The twelfth Music and Speech Festival in 1969 featured "a beautifully controlled exhibition of cello playing" from Raphael Wallfisch in his last performance as a schoolboy. The school play became a regular feature of the school year. Commenting upon the production of the second half of the *York Mystery Plays* and *Philoctetes* in the spring of 1962, *The Latymerian* noted that "it is a matter of satisfaction that boys who can give us the Jantaculum in one term can give us plays of this kind in the next". From the pages of the school magazine come glimpses of future distinguished acting careers, such as Alan Rickman's performance as Sir Epicure Mammon in *The Alchemist* in 1964 whose "lazy and smug drawl, affected movements and lucid, well-pointed verse speaking succeeded well for this avaricious yet perversely sensitive booby", and Mel Smith's *Falstaff* in 1970, when the reviewer wrote that he had "rarely seen a more vivid and consistent characterisation of this great role" and considered it "the best individual performance I have seen at Latymer". The Gild, under the direction of its ebullient Reve, Wilf Sharp, who took over the post from R C Davies in 1959, together with its junior versions, went from strength to strength. In 1962 it celebrated its 40th anniversary with a dinner attended by 200 Gildani, including the first two Reves, Skinner and Davies, at Hammersmith Town Hall. The Gild then had 180 members but it was pointed out that "thousands of Latymerians have experienced that indefinable blend of gaiety, artistic purpose and sheer hard work which goes to make up the Gild spirit". Once a Gildanus, always a Gildanus, and Old Latymerians protected the Gild with a fierce jealousy. Reviewing the 1971 Jantaculum, which was perhaps not the best of recent years, Alan Rickman wrote that "the Jantaculum is a marvellous old monster and it's sad to see it slip; it won't mind being shaken up now and then, but treat it with respect. This thing is bigger than all of us". The wide variety of other societies waxed and waned with the fashion of the times but Latymer boys hardly ever had a dull moment. One innovation was the beginnings in the late 1950s of what is now known as Activities Week which provides an enormous range of activities for most of the school in the fallow period after examinations at the end of the summer term. It began as an effort by the head of PE, Mike Bond, to find something for boys to do who had just finished their O levels. He took parties each year to Plas y Brenyn in Wales where the boys enjoyed walking, canoeing and mountaineering. Later, when a change of examination boards altered the timing of the summer exams, the rest of the school had to be catered for and Activities Week burgeoned. Foreign travel continued and more boys than ever travelled abroad each year to a greater range of other locations, Greece being particularly popular. The relationship with schools in Germany and France remained strong. In 1965, for instance, the BBC recorded two separate contests of *Top of the Form* between Latymer Upper and the Johanneum in the school hall, one in English, which Latymer won by 38–31, and the other in German, which was tied.

Top of the Form, *recorded by the BBC at the school in 1965.*

The boat club gained a second boat, the "K E S", in 1960 and continued to flourish, its successes including winning the Public Schools Race at the Marlow Regatta. Cricket prospered under the guidance of another professional coach until the governors decided after three seasons that they could no longer afford him. The growing size of the school led to the organisation in 1965 of separate sports days for the three different parts of the school. Cycling was introduced as a competitive sport in 1969 when the school won the national ten-mile championship at the first attempt.

The spiritual life of the school was not neglected. Kenneth Sutcliffe was a man of strong Christian convictions and a licensed lay reader in the Church of England. When John Evans became school chaplain in 1958 in succession to Monty Cann, who had died after a long illness bravely borne earlier in the year, changes were made which saw communion celebrated each week in the school chapel and weekly intercessions organised by the Christian Fellowship. Social service was eventually encouraged in the late 1960s when boys undertook tasks assigned to them by the Hammersmith welfare services department in a quiet and unobtrusive way.

It should not be thought that the path of corporate life ran smoothly at the school throughout this period. As the 1960s went on, young people everywhere were beginning to rebel against the conventions of previous generations, to display more self-confidence and express doubts about previously unquestioned certainties. Latymer Upper did not escape entirely from this new attitude (most notoriously perhaps several boys were contributors to the *Schoolkids' Oz*) although it manifested itself in a much more restrained way than in many other places. The major casualty was the school cadet corps, which had been commanded with distinction since the end of the war by Lt. Col. Tom Stewart, MC, also an Old Latymerian, who had seen distinguished service in North Africa. The school had never had a strong corps tradition and the cadet corps at the school had always had its ups and downs from the time of its institution in 1905. During the 1960s the reaction among the young against militarism led to the corps' final demise at Latymer. Numbers dwindled away and the corps was no longer sufficiently strong to justify its existence. It was wound up in the summer of 1966. By now the few opportunities given to boys to mix with the girls from Godolphin were seen as frustrating rather than liberating. There had been attempts in the early 1960s to establish a sixth form association with Godolphin and Latymer for the organisation of more joint activities. But this seems to have come to naught since an article in the school magazine in 1967, while applauding the school's links with the Johanneum and the Lycée Marcelin Berthelot at St Maur overseas and, through the activities of the Freston Society, with schools at home, deplored the lack of contact with the girls at Godolphin: "it must surely be impossible to educate one fully and give a reasonable representation of life in an all-male society". As a result more co-operation did indeed begin between the two schools, with girls from Godolphin participating in the Latymer productions of *Oh, What a Lovely War!* and *Trial by Jury* in 1969. The 1967 issue of *The Latymerian* also included a letter which paraded a more general frustration with the way the school was run. The writer insisted that the school did not prepare boys for life, adding with youthful overstatement that "often this school

110

seems to encourage people not to think". School rules were inflexible and there should be greater consultation with the school on how it should be run, the letter going on to recite a long list of areas for review. The headmaster himself recognised the changes taking place among sixth formers, the greater consciousness of their own group identity, their perception of themselves as more adult, their susceptibility to outside influences. He remarked that "The attitude and outlook of boys changed more rapidly than it used to". A sixth form committee was the result of this meeting of minds. Coming together regularly with senior staff, it succeeded in making uniform optional for the sixth form although conditions were imposed which would ensure, in the headmaster's words, "that the urge towards self-expression in clothes should not go too far". The committee was one of several reasons why the rebellious sixties did not cause many problems at Latymer Upper. Kenneth Sutcliffe's quiet but firm example as headmaster, always listening and never inflexible, with a shrewd understanding of how the boys felt, was another. The Gild, which brought together masters and boys in a way unparalleled in most other schools, was a safety valve for letting off steam. One writer compared the Jantaculum to Shakespeare's *Twelfth Night*: "if the roles of masters and pupils are not exactly reversed, they are at least equal".

The 1960s were also a time of educational uncertainty for the school as it became unfashionable for local education authorities to send scholars to schools outside the state system. The LCC began reducing the number of places it took in 1960, ostensibly because of falling school rolls, an excuse of which the governors were suspicious. When Middlesex followed suit in 1963, the head recommended increasing the school's entry at age nine to maintain recruitment standards. With the creation of the GLC, the ILEA and the borough education authorities in the mid-1960s, the governors began to grow concerned at the reluctance of the boroughs to commit themselves to take up places at the school. The boroughs teamed up to create a joint scheme to take up free places until the end of the decade and the ILEA, although recognising the tension between a reorganisation of schools along comprehensive lines alongside purely selective schools, also stated that it would be taking free places for some time to come, albeit on a reduced scale. The head and the chairman of governors emphasised at that time (1966) "the school's wish to be closely linked with the local authorities' provision of education. They would not want the school to become independent". While the head was willing to extend the range of entry if that would enable the ILEA to take up more free places, he insisted that any entrants should be of good academic ability since it would be unacceptable to make the school less attractive to fee-paying parents. This was particularly important since the direct grant now formed a smaller part of school income, the result of which had been an increase in fees from £69 a year in 1958 to £210 in 1971. The future of the direct grant system was under constant review in political and educational circles and Kenneth Sutcliffe was one of those who submitted evidence to the Public Schools Commission whose second report in 1970 recommended either the continuation of the system with the reorganisation of direct grant schools along comprehensive lines or the gradual elimination of the system and a move by the schools towards independence. Nevertheless by the autumn term of 1971, although the ILEA had now stopped taking up places, there was still a high level of free places at Latymer Upper, with

Colin Turner, Head of Middle School, the writer and producer of many Jantacula.

111

Opposite page: *The rear entrance to the Prep School gardens* (above), *and* (below) *the playground and sports hall.*

Arthur Abbott, head of physics from 1948–66. His pupils established an outstanding record of university entrance awards.

109 allocated to new entrants. That characteristic feature of the school, its class-lessness, which failed to recognise any distinction between scholarship boys and non-scholarship boys, remained as strong as ever.

It should be pointed out that during this period the school recorded the greatest academic successes of its history. In 1960 22 university awards were gained, followed by 20 in 1961, while in 1962 32 Latymerians obtained places at Oxbridge. An extra day's holiday was granted in recognition of these results. Of 150 leavers in 1964, 80 of them were taking places at university, 32 of those at Oxbridge. In 1969 boys won seven Oxbridge awards and 12 places. Such results reflected great credit upon the staff. From 1948 until his retirement in 1966, Arthur Abbott was the head of physics. In the tradition of Latymer science masters, he too had designed and made much of the laboratory apparatus, planned the layout of the new laboratories, and written a world-wide best-selling O level text book. John Howard, the Old Latymerian head of maths, concentrated mainly upon teaching the third year sixth and had a brilliant record of success. Another Old Latymerian, Colin Turner, who had joined the English department in 1957, was an exceptional actor, drama teacher and producer. The personalities of Wilf Sharp and George Offiler were still casting a warm glow over the English and history departments.

Kenneth Sutcliffe retired at the end of the summer term of 1971. The governors recorded that "By his integrity, his reliability and his general stewardship, he had ensured that the best traditions of Latymer had been upheld". This was a general verdict. On his death in 1991 his obituary in *The Latymerian* commented that "he left the school in good heart and shape ... It was well-adjusted to the changes that had taken place under his direction, but an essential spirit, ethos and *esprit de corps* ... had been preserved".

Mr Harman conducting the choir in a broadcast from the Great Hall, 1956.

CHAPTER EIGHT

'Respect, Tradition and Innovation'

PAST AND PRESENT

1971–1995

Maurice Isaac was 42 when he took over as the fifth headmaster of the Latymer Upper School. After attending Selhurst Grammar School in Croydon, he had read history at Magdalene College, Cambridge. Teaching had taken him to Liverpool Collegiate School and then Bristol Grammar School, where the rigid academic pursuit of the very best results from the very best pupils to the detriment of others convinced him that there must be a better way. He then moved to Colchester Royal Grammar School, where he was head of history, before an appointment as headmaster of Yeovil School, a boys' grammar school, in 1966. Arriving at Latymer Upper, he was delighted to find that, as he had hoped, it had neither school song nor a cadet corps nor houses.

As a headmaster Isaac was efficient, business-like and clear-cut. He knew what he wanted and he knew how to get it. In his first term at Latymer Isaac wrote in *The Latymerian* that "I do believe in planning from existing situations rather than from hypothetical circumstances. At the same time, I know the direction in which I want to move and I try to use each opportunity as it is presented to move onwards in that direction". As one former member of staff recalled, "He was a man who had definite ideas, positive ideas, much more forthright than any of his predecessors". This did not endear him to his staff in the first instance: "It was a bit like having a cold bath for a lot of us". They had lived through a more relaxed era when outside pressures upon the school had not been so great. On the other hand, it was also said that it took the new head some time to get used to his new school. He came from a well-run but smaller grammar school in Somerset, which had not yet been touched by the adolescent discontent of the late 1960s, to take over a West London grammar school of more than a thousand boys, quite a few of whom were scruffy, loud and independent. But, as his staff found that their headmaster was the better for knowing, so Maurice Isaac came to appreciate the school as he settled in.

For the lower half of the school he was very much in the traditional mould of headmasters, distant, severe and aloof. This impression changed as boys progressed through the school. He was an excellent teacher of history (in the tradition of many Latymerian staff he had already produced a text book which went

Opposite page (above): Music and economics departments, with the art department in the background. This area is scheduled to become a performing arts centre. (Below): Interior of the library.

Maurice Isaac, Headmaster 1971–1988.

The Great Hall, 1971.

into three editions) and was held in "terrific affection" by those he taught. His lessons could be lively for he had a very physical way of teaching: boys recall, for instance, the way he demonstrated the Schlieffen Plan by using individual boys to represent the nation states of Europe. He had "an unfailing ability to put a name to a face". The story is told of Isaac greeting by name one boy in the second year on the first occasion that he had met him since the boy had sat the entrance examination.

Soon after he had been appointed he set out a philosophy which was not far removed from those of the previous two headmasters:

> When I was appointed, the question I dearly wanted to know the answer to was this: "Is it possible to run a highly academic school in which the most able are stretched to their finest achievements without creating a sense of failure or inferiority in those who are only slightly less able?"
>
> Even were a balance to be achieved, I think that critics would still accuse the school of thinking only in terms of its potential Oxbridge scholars.
>
> I would rather try to provide for the needs of each individual and to recognise each individual's particular qualities. One shouldn't confuse academic success at a particular stage of a person's education either with eternal virtues or even with worldly success or usefulness to the community.

With all this in mind changes were made to the curriculum within the first year of Maurice Isaac's appointment. The sixth form curriculum was broadened with the introduction of business studies and politics. The sixth form general studies programme was rearranged to enable occasional lectures to be given, usually from distinguished speakers, such as Peter Walker (an Old Latymerian), Trevor Huddleston and Lord Goodman. Below the sixth form, Isaac believed that there was no point in streaming boys whose very entry into an academic school was an indication of their ability. Instead, five parallel forms were created in which boys were grouped, not according to the position they had gained in the entrance examination, but in relation to a variety of other factors, such as where they lived, how they travelled to school, and where they had previously been to school. At a higher level there was setting in some subjects and after the second year there was still one fast O level stream. The only compulsory O levels were to be English, French and mathematics. Isaac regarded end of term or end of year exams in the Lower School as a waste of time and instead placed greater emphasis upon the continuous testing, correcting and assessment of work throughout the year. Reports were issued termly with each subject graded according to effort and achievement. Form and subject orders became a thing of the past.

The most pressing concern of the time, however, was the future of the direct grant system. When Maurice Isaac was appointed headmaster, more than half the pupils held free places from various local education authorities. The remaining places were held by fee-paying pupils, although fees themselves were low since the school received a capitation grant for each boy from the Department of Education and Science, as it was now known. Since many fee-payers were also eligible for the remission of fees, depending upon their income, in effect few parents paid fees and the fees they paid were often small. In the early 1970s, however, more and more local education authorities were no longer taking free places at the school. There was the possibility that the school would lose the direct grant should the number of free places fall below a quarter of the annual intake, so the governors agreed that if necessary fees would have to rise to cover the cost of the places the governors themselves would have to offer to retain the grant. At the same time, however, the Department of Education was reluctant to approve increases in fees during a period when inflation and costs were rising rapidly. At least at Latymer Upper finance was never a worry, thanks to the growing wealth of the Foundation, whose property assets were appreciating considerably and whose sale proceeds invested on the money markets were earning considerable sums in interest. But the combination of greater control over fees by the Department and a declining number of LEA free places placed a question mark over the survival of the direct grant system which was emphasised by the growing political campaign against it. In 1975 the Labour Government announced that the system would be phased out from 1 September 1976.

The end of the direct grant system, therefore, posed a threat to the make-up of the school. It did pose a question mark over the continuation of the Latymer tradition, which could perhaps be defined as the provision of an academic education in a tolerant and liberal environment for boys of all backgrounds regardless of financial means. For while many of those who would have benefited from the direct grant system would be able to afford school fees, inevitably there were bound to be those who could not. Although the governors began an appeal fund (which was administered by the head of economics, Derek Bone) which was partly intended to fund bursaries for the future, the level of assistance expected to be provided by bursaries would never compare with the help which the direct grant system had given. The headmaster and the governors recognised that inevitably independence would make a Latymer Upper a predominantly fee-paying school.

Independence, however, was really the only option open to the governors. Given the wealth of the Foundation, it was a viable alternative. Closure was pointless. As a local comprehensive, even if that had been philosophically acceptable, the school's survival was also questionable, given the fact that few of its pupils now came from Hammersmith and most came from other areas of London where there were ample places for them in local schools. Some Old Latymerians found independence difficult to accept because of the inevitability that most pupils would now be fee-payers. One member of staff left because he could not agree with the decision. On the other hand, one governor appointed by one of the local Labour councils who was also an Old Latymerian voted in favour of independence and then resigned from the party.

When the chance came in 1981, however, for the school to participate in the assisted places scheme, Latymer Upper had no hesitation. Ted Philips, the chairman of governors, was himself an Old Latymerian, who, in his own words, "was always anxious to maintain the structure as far as possible of fee paying and subsidised places and was therefore delighted when the assisted places scheme came to complement our own bursary scheme". By 1981, there were still direct grant boys at the school, although only in the sixth form. The assisted places scheme presented the opportunity to rescusitate the tradition at Latymer of a school where at any one time since before the First World War some 40% of the school roll had benefited from state assistance of one sort or another. It was regarded as "an important step towards a more socially integrated Latymer". Under the new scheme, individual schools agreed directly with the Department of Education on the number of places to be made available. All places were subject to a means test and the school received no capitation grant. The Department still retained control over the level of fees. Latymer Upper applied to offer 100 places out of 150 available at the school each year for 11 year olds. The Department agreed on 45 places a year, which still represented a greater number than almost any other school taking part in the scheme. In fact, in the autumn of 1981, when the scheme began, 49 boys entered the school with the help of assisted places. The school roll totalled 1,059 boys, of whom 34% were there with the benefit of financial assistance of one kind or another: 49 under the assisted places scheme, 124 with governors' bursaries, and the final 191 boys from the direct grant scheme. The number of boys with bursaries fell sharply as the school embraced the assisted places scheme. At the beginning of Maurice Isaac's last year in office, out of 1,015 boys at the school, only 10 received bursaries compared to 289 with assisted places (28%).

The school's popularity never waned. There was always considerable competition for places in the school at 9 (for the preparatory department) and 11 (for

Front of the school on King Street, early 1980s.

the main school). Although there were suggestions from time to time that boys should also be taken at 8 and 13, the headmaster saw no reason to do so. At both those ages he believed that the school would be in competition with other prep schools and other independent schools, as a result of which the chance was that Latymer would no longer be the first choice of many of those seeking admission. At 9 and 11, on the other hand, there was less competition from other schools yet a continuing high level of demand for places which ensured that admission standards could be maintained. This showed in the examination results over the years. On average 22 boys each year won awards or places to Oxbridge. The best such results came in 1971–72 (31) and 1980–81 (31), although there was a slight falling off in the late 1980s. Oxbridge awards were abolished from the mid-1980s onwards and with them went the third year sixth, for so many years a characteristic of the school. Besides Oxbridge places, of course, should not be forgotten the countless places at other universities and places of higher education attained by Latymer boys. O and A level pass rates hovered around 85–90% and were to improve further in the years ahead.

But, as with Wilkinson and Sutcliffe, academic excellence was never the only goal for Maurice Isaac. What one old boy has called the "extraordinarily rich life" of extra-curricular activities which had been a tradition at the school since the late 1930s remained abundantly in evidence during his headship. Drama and music in particular flourished. Of the many fine drama productions over the years, a fleeting glimpse of a future star is caught in the review of *The Caucasian Chalk Circle* in 1977 when a central role was taken by Hugh Grant who "acted well and enlisted our sympathy but overdid the moustache and the

Right: *The Curia of the Gild in about 1974.* Below: *Drama in the 1970s. The bottom picture shows a Jantaculum.*

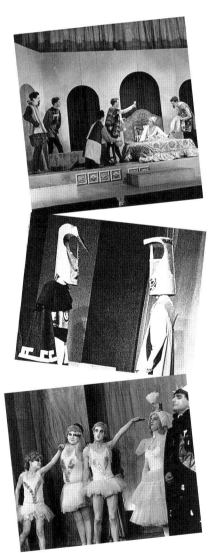

dumbness"; and again in 1978 when as Wagner in *Doctor Faustus* he was "outstanding. The evil inherent in this character ... came across brilliantly. His diction and timing were, likewise, first-class". Clifford Harman retired in 1976 but the development of music in the school continued to develop under the direction of his successors, Shane Fletcher and Richard Hobson. By the late 1970s, musical life at the school included a joint orchestra with the Godolphin & Latymer School (whose first concert featured Beethoven's Choral Symphony), a junior orchestra, a string group and string quartet, a piano trio, two clarinet ensembles, the chamber choir and an early music group. Debating was revived throughout the school. A new sixth form society was established, the Forum Society, which attracted an array of distinguished speakers.

The Gild remained a considerable influence. It celebrated its 50th anniversary in 1972 with another celebratory dinner in the Town Hall attended by 240 people. The BBC drama producer and Old Latymerian, Shaun Sutton, replied on behalf of the guests and spoke of "the Gild's over-riding influence in his life". Ten years later it successfully reached the age of 60. For many the Jantaculum continued to symbolise "all that Latymer stands for: the all too rare relationship and mutual respect of master and boy". Maurice Isaac, as Custos, and his second master, George Terry, became well-known for the cameo appearances they made in the annual Jantacula. *The Latymerian* in the summer of 1973 reveals that in the final morowspeche "A swivel chair swung round and we were faced by our controversial Custos in the guise of a particularly controversial film director. Blue suede shoes, blue denim shirt, cool shades and a curly grey wig all contributed to this remarkable transformation". By the late 1970s, girls from Godolphin were taking a regular part in Gild activities. Wilf Sharp was succeeded as Reve by the irrepressible Fred Mayo. In turn, he handed over the reins as Reve in 1985 to the head of the English department, Chris Owens, who believed strongly in the central importance of the Gild. Upon his departure for another post two years later, another Old Latymerian reared in the ways of the Gild, Colin Turner, took over the post. Turner, with Edward Stead, had written, produced, and acted in many Jantacula, in which his performances as the dame in the pantomime which usually made up the second half became renowned. Under Chris Hammond, more and more boys at the school took part in the Duke of Edinburgh Award Scheme, with the first of the school's many Gold

Awards being won by Simon Tye, Ludomir Serafin and David Hull in 1978.

Scouting prospered under the leadership of John Butterworth. Activities Week, involving almost the entire school, took boys all over the country as well as abroad on walking, climbing, sailing, canoeing, camping and sundry other expeditions. The foreign exchange visits continued and for the first time Godolphin girls joined Latymer boys on the visit to the Lycée Jean de la Fontaine in Paris in 1987.

Jim Clark took over as coach of the boat club after Alan Watson left the school in 1974. Like his predecessor, Jim Clark was an international oarsman and was part of the silver-medal-winning British eight in the 1976 Montreal Olympics. Perhaps the most successful team of this period was that which came third in the national junior U16 coxed fours in 1976, came second in the Beale Cup for 2nd VIIIs in the national schools championships in 1977, and won some 16 regattas in between, as well as being selected to row for England in the Home Countries International Regatta in Wales in 1978. It was said that Jim Clark, after whom the new eight was named which arrived in 1978, "took this group, mostly rugby club dropouts and unfit, uncoordinated sporting failures and moulded them, through intensive training and coaching, into one of the most successful group of sportsmen Latymer has ever produced". One of those rugby club dropouts was Andy Holmes, who subsequently went on to win two Olympic gold medals and one Olympic bronze medals.and two world championship titles. Other boat club successes also included the national junior quad sculls gold medal in 1985. Sailing became an option for summer sporting activities. Golf was both popular and successful in competition, the school providing the independent schools golf champion, John Cowgill, in 1986. Athletics underwent a resurgence. Football was still very popular and the school reached the final of the Ebdon Trophy in 1986. Latymer rugby players were regularly selected for county honours and occasionally for international schoolboy honours, as were Latymer badminton and squash players. The most outstanding schoolboy cricketers of the period were Richard Hayward and Simon Hughes, who both went on to play county cricket. The Wood Lane ground was taken to a peak of condition rarely seen before, helped by new drainage works, while the new sports hall and swimming pool acquired by the school in the late 1970s opened up new opportunities for boys. The school at one stage even had the country's most active tiddlywinks team!

Sports in the 1970s. From top: *Badminton; middle school sports day at Wood Lane, 1979; the new swimming pool of 1976.* Left: *Old Latymerians vs. school at the C J Smith memorial sports ground at Whitton.*

The new swimming pool and sports hall were part of the continuing rebuilding programme which Maurice Isaac had inherited from his predecessor. The programme was not set immutably. The economic chaos of the time, with soaring inflation and recurrent recessions which sent many builders on each occasion out of business (including the one who worked upon the new sports hall), meant that the governors had to be flexible both in terms of what they wanted and when they wanted it. The original intention with the phase nearing completion during the mid-1970s had been for a complex comprising swimming pool, sports hall and squash courts. The latter had to be omitted since it was not possible to obtain permission to demolish Latymer House on which site they would have been erected. The first building to have been built was the sports hall but it was considered wiser at a time of high inflation to build the most expensive building, the swimming pool, first. This was a decision which did not go down well in some quarters, which was hardly surprising since the old gymnasium had been too small since 1963. On the other hand, at least the school had a gymnasium. For the previous two years the boys had been unable to do much swimming because of problems at the Lime Grove baths. The school's four lane 25 metre pool was completed on Christmas Eve 1975. The school timetable was altered to provide a period in the pool for every boy in the school, and its uses extended from swimming and water-polo to sub-aqua and canoeing. The pool alone cost some £300,000 when the sum for the whole group of buildings had originally been estimated at £70,000! The sports hall which followed was finally completed in early 1980 and was opened by a distinguished Old Latymerian, the Solicitor General, Sir Ian Percival, MP, on 13 June that year. With the gymnasium finally free for conversion, it was possible to embark upon the creation of

Right: *The new sports hall under construction, 1980.* Above: *Sir Ian Percival, Solicitor-General, at the opening of the building later that year.*

the new library, again a facility which the school was very much in need of. In 18 months the imaginative conversion had been completed and the new library was opened by Joan Bakewell on 25 November 1981. The old library accommodation was given over to the biology department.

The development plan for the school was now 16 years old and, after the completion of the library, the headmaster decided that the time had come to review it. The original strategy had been followed with little deviation so far but in 1965 it had been estimated that all the phases of the plan would be completed by 1970 at a cost not exceeding £500,000. By 1981 only half of them had been achieved at almost twice that sum. The next part of the plan envisaged the extension of the ABC block to form a new chemistry department, the demolition of the main corridors and the erection of a new classroom block, and the demolition of the hall and its replacement by two new halls and a new administration block. The rehousing of the departments involved, chemistry, geography and history, was likely to cost a million pounds. Maurice Isaac believed that the existing accommodation was quite satisfactory and that the money would be better spent upon refurbishment. The demolition of the hall was no longer a possibility. Planning consent was unlikely while the brave new world of industrialised building which had swept aside many magnificent buildings during the 1960s and early 1970s had come to an end and was being replaced by greater awareness of the nation's existing architectural heritage. The governors agreed. By the summer of 1982, the hall had been magnificently refurbished, revealing for the first time in many years the honey colour of the unglazed brickwork and the contrasting salmon pink of the brickwork framing the window arches, and the King Street screen had been cleaned. The hall became a sixth form concourse with studies, common and recreation rooms. One consequence of this was that the hall was no longer available for drama so the school play and the Jantaculum were moved across the road to the theatre of the Polish Cultural Centre. The main corridor classrooms were refurbished. The New Building, now known as E block, was upgraded and the space between E block and the hall was to become a new entrance lobby and exhibition hall. The chemistry classrooms and laboratories would be modernised. A small concert hall was also to be converted from

Lower Fifth drawing group in the art department.

The traditional and the modern. Pottery with Mr Pye (left), *and* (right) *history lesson in one of the classrooms designed by Hans Henlein, the school architect.*

Wilfred Sharp, head of English and Reve of the Gild.

Soccer and rugby thrived at the school in the 1980s. The central figure in the picture on the right is Simon Henderson, later Captain of Rosslyn Park.

the existing craftshop. The entire cost of the exercise was intended to be borne by the Foundation. One alteration made to this revised plan was the creation of a Craft Design & Technology facility within the south block of the school. The displaced classics department was then transferred to a new floor built above the new library. The new CDT centre was opened by Maurice Isaac in the autumn of 1988, the term after his retirement from the headship.

Isaac had taken charge of the Latymer Upper School at a time when it required a firm hand on the tiller. Together with his like-minded chairman of governors, Ted Philips, he had steered the school through the end of the direct grant system, through independence and into the assisted places scheme. His achievement can perhaps be best summed up firstly through the words of a parent and secondly through his own words. At the beginning of December 1976, the headmaster received a letter from a parent whose son was leaving the school at the end of that term. The letter spoke of the headmaster's approachability and sense of humour, which "has never failed as far as we are concerned to get the message across in the pleasantest possible way", and commented that "it seems to us that every member of the staff has been responsible for ensuring that his [their son's] years at Latymer have been a time of happiness and fulfilment". Perhaps most revealingly the letter went on to say that

> In these troubled and bewildering educational times it has been a considerable relief to us to know that he was at a school where the standards were not falling, where the code of moral values which we have done our best to instil into our children was being maintained by you, too, and where so much genuine good will and understanding exists on the part of the staff towards the boys.

Several years after leaving the school, Maurice Isaac, in writing about the retirement of George Terry as second master, commented on their starring roles in the annual Jantaculum: "Those days of Jantaculum epitomised so much that I found enjoyable about Latymer. There was fun but there was professionalism, there was a friendly, relaxed atmosphere but there was respect, tradition and innovation". For all this Isaac must take his share of the credit.

Credit must also be given for the part played in this achievement by the Latymer staff. Several long-serving members who had made a particular contri-

bution to the school over the years retired during the latter part of Maurice Isaac's time. Wilf Sharp, known at one time or another as "Toffee", had imparted his great love of literature to several generations of Latymerians. One former pupil remembered that this very individual master keenly believed that something could only be well taught if the teacher himself appreciated implicitly its true value. This meant that authors Wilf Sharp had no time for rarely found their way into his classroom while he devoted all his passion and enthusiasm to those for whom he had genuine admiration. Wilf Sharp's contribution to the school lay not only in his teaching. He masterminded the success of the Gild for many years as its Reve and threw himself wholeheartedly into Latymer's artistic life, acting, singing, producing plays and a host of other things.

George Offiler, known to many as "Bert", the erudite and eloquent head of history, retired at the same time as Wilf Sharp. Again he was responsible for igniting within many of the pupils who passed through his hands an interest in his subject which came from his own deep love for it. He never had a narrow view of history and always encouraged his pupils to broaden their historical perspective. He too made a valuable contribution to the life of the Gild, for many years occupying the post of Publick Oratour Emeritus with a "silver-tongued solemnity". One former pupil echoed the views of many others when he recalled that George Offiler was "an unforgettable example to us all". Geoffrey Grimsey, who had been responsible for the introduction of rugby at Latymer after the Second World War, was another all-rounder, master, actor, director, singer, sportsman, sailor and Reve of the Gild, who retired during this period. He led the classics department for many years while at the same time transforming the school's careers service. As Reve he brought "his wit, style and inventive ideas to many Jantacula and morowspeches". In Geoffrey Grimsey, who had dedicated "his many talents, his abundant energy and his high standards" to the school, Latymer had been well served as by so many other members of staff past and present.

Another such was John Howard, whose talents extended not only to the perpetuation of the tradition excellence in the school's mathematics department but also to coaching the boat club for many years and leading parties of boys on skiing and sailing expeditions. Fred Mayo not only taught mathematics and physics, he served as an officer in the corps until its disbandment, he coached both soccer and cricket, he was a dedicated Reve of the Gild, and one of the most colourful characters at the school. John Spong and Norman Edmundson had been the *eminences grises* behind the Latymer French department for many years. Michael Bond, for many years head of PE and then, in his final period at Latymer, head of the craft department, had also run Activities Week, helped with the Duke of Edinburgh's Award Scheme, played violin and saxophone in the school orchestra and the Jantacuband, and built sets for plays. Activities Week had been started in the first place by Laurence Elliott who had been a distinguished head of geography at the school for many years. This fact was recognised externally by his appointment as a chief examiner in the subject at A level and as a Fellow of the Royal Geographical Society as well as by the subsequent successful academic careers of many of his own pupils. In addition, he was involved in coaching cricket at the school and in leading several parties on educational

Maurice Isaac, invited to speak at the 450th anniversary of the Johanneum, emphasising the strong links with the school.

Fred Mayo, physics and mathematics teacher and Reve of the Gild, umpiring on a wet afternoon.

The choir performing in the Great Hall, about 1979.

cruises. The 36 years Tony Hull spent at Latymer from 1950 were divided between the English department and the prep department, where he became head in 1971. In that role he was firm but fair, caring about all his pupils and the school, earning their respect and admiration. Football was his main interest outside the classroom and for 19 years he coached the school first team.

It should not be thought, however, that the departure of so many who had made such an invaluable collective contribution to the school left a denuded staff room. Latymer is a school which many of those who join the teaching staff find difficult to leave. It stimulates them to give of their best consistently not only in class but outside their teaching roles. At any one time the continuity of this tradition upon the staff is represented by a core who have served the school for the best part of their teaching careers and mention might be made of those who fill that role today, such as Peter Cotmore, Graham Bearman, Malcolm Stansbie, Bruce Perkins, Chris Hammond, Peter Stevens, Robert Orme, Martin Willson, Geoffrey Tait and Tony Fella, all of whom were appointed in the 1960s and are current members of staff.

Maurice Isaac's successor inherited a highly successful school well-placed to adapt to the social and educational changes to come. Martin Pavey had not come straight into teaching. After leaving Magdalen College School in Oxford, he had worked in shipping for five years, taking his A levels during that time on his own initiative. He then went on to obtain an MA in English at London University and was 27 when he began teaching at Lancing College. His first headship came at 35 and at the time of his appointment as headmaster of Latymer Upper he was head of Cranbrook School in Kent.

Martin Pavey, Headmaster 1988–1991.

Like all independent schools, Latymer Upper was facing great changes in education. It was an era when a headmaster was seen more as *primus inter pares*, when there was much more emphasis upon pastoral care in schools, when schools were being run more democratically. The independent sector was becoming much more competitive, as a result of which headmasters for the first time were compelled to draw up marketing strategies to avoid being squeezed out of the market. Over the next few years, as government policy shifted, competition would also come from autonomous grant maintained schools in the public sector and question marks would be raised about the future of the assisted places scheme. Value for money and greater accountability would therefore become more of a consideration than ever before.

Martin Pavey was particularly concerned to carry on improvements to the fabric of the school, and to enhance the facilities it had to offer. In terms of the continuing building programme, the headmaster wanted to see appropriate accommodation for the chemistry department, which had been outstanding for some time, and suggested that a new building might be the best way forward. He also wanted to see a more presentable school office and reception area, better social and dining accommodation for staff and pupils (especially the sixth form), and, ultimately, a school theatre. These recommendations, he told the governors, would "provide us with considerable extra quality which I feel we need to compete in today's market. More important, it would greatly enhance our teaching and the lives of our children".

The financing of this programme exercised the governors' minds considerably, their major concerns being the effect any increase in fees would have and the need to secure the future income of the Foundation, given the considerable sums spent over the last decade upon the school. There was the possibility of disposing of Wood Lane and using the resulting funds not only to purchase larger playing fields but also to finance the head's proposals. But the disposal of the Wood Lane land always remained problematical and eventually the board would agree in 1993 that the refurbishment of the changing rooms there could wait no longer. Instead it was agreed to modernise the chemistry department, provide additional ground floor accommodation, and install an additional floor in the ample roof space above it to create more classrooms for the English department. As part of a further internal reorganisation of space, much of the ABC teaching block would be refurbished at the same time.

It was a time of change in the staff room. The saddest change was the sudden death of Colin Turner in early 1990. He was then head of middle school and Reve of the Gild, as well as being an outstanding member of the English department. The theatre was his great love and he was intimately involved with anything to do with drama at Latymer. Besides his skills as a director, producer

The entrance to the staff room.

Revd Glyn Iball, chaplain 1971–1992.

and scriptwriter, he was himself a consummate actor. On one occasion, when the boy playing Sir Andrew Aguecheek in a production of *Twelfth Night* was incapacitated through spraining his ankle, Colin Turner took his place at the next performance, giving a word-perfect and sparkling rendition of the role. Drama was not his only strength. He contributed wholeheartedly to many other school activities. George Terry recalled that "He was a good disciplinarian because he was always understanding, fair and kind." He played a central role in the charity work undertaken by the school, not only in organising much of the fund-raising which went on but also in giving up time during his vacations for several years, together with the school chaplain, to take 30 disadvantaged Hammersmith children away on a week's holiday. He had a wonderful sense of humour, which on one occasion, when George Terry asked for his help in providing a design for his new office, saw Colin Turner transform it into "Chez George", as a French café complete with checked table cloths, cutlery, wine, candles, menus and plates of *hors d'oeuvre*. Without question he had a considerable influence upon the school. Wilf Sharp, his former head of department, remarked that "Everything he touched was filled with his own enthusiasm but also tempered with his critical judgement, respected by all, resented by none". A fifth form pupil wrote that his death had "emphasised the important role he played in holding together Latymer Upper School". It was a severe loss to the school to lose so suddenly in his prime one who was so utterly committed to the school.

Several other stalwart members of staff said their goodbyes at the end of the summer term following Colin Turner's sad death. George Terry, the second master, whom many boys remember for his firm and fair running of the school, retired after over 40 years of distinguished service. His unrivalled knowledge of the school enabled him to ease the transition through many changes with calm efficiency. He also enabled many generations of boys and staff to fulfil their

ambitions. John Butterworth, the head of the lower school under whose influence Latymer Upper had developed a flourishing scout troop since 1972, departed,
together with John Carroll, head of classics between 1977 and 1990 who had
reintroduced Latin at A level as well as Greek, and Andrew Douglas, the head
of English.

The board of governors, under the chairmanship of J G Emms and then Dr
J Edelman, was also changing both in its composition and its operation. They
built upon the good work already done by Ted Philips who had reduced the
number of main board meetings to once a term in favour of more detailed
monthly meetings of the finance committee and introduced greater financial
discipline. Now there were many new, often younger, members with a wider mix
of skills.

*Colin Diggory, Headmaster since
1991.*

Martin Pavey left the school at Easter 1991. His successor was Colin
Diggory, who had succeeded George Terry as second master in 1990, the first
time that the post had been advertised externally. He had been educated at Sir
William Turner's, Redcar, and at Durham University, where he graduated with
a first class degree in mathematics. He had taught at Manchester Grammar
School, St Paul's, and latterly at Merchant Taylors', where he had been head of
Mathematics Side. Coming to Latymer Upper, he too had recognised what
Martin Pavey had seen, a school which, because of the assisted places scheme,
had not yet come to terms with what it meant to be an independent school in a
competitive fee-paying environment.

There was concern about the over-reliance of the school upon the assisted
places scheme, whose future was uncertain. The weakness of the scheme was
that the parents of many able boys neither knew about the scheme nor how to
apply for it because of the understandable hostility of many primary schools
towards it. It was therefore covering only a part of the school population which
had previously been served by the direct grant system. There was also concern
about the school's undeveloped relationships with private prep schools. With the
changes in the educational climate the time was now right for the school's
preparatory department to compete with other prep schools for boys entering at
their usual age of eight. At 11 the school took more boys than many other
schools at a time when competition was increasing with other schools at that
age, both in the independent and state sector. There was always a danger that
boys would be admitted who would not normally have gained entry and therefore in diluting the school's academic standards. The alternative, however, of
competing for the best boys entering the independent sector from private prep
schools at the age of 13, was possible for Latymer Upper only if it reduced its
intake at the age of 11.

*Dr J Edelman, CBE, DSc,
Chairman of the Latymer Foundation
since 1990.*

Colin Diggory was firmly of the opinion that entry at 13, as well as at 8, was
an essential part of the school's future. In addition, the financial burden to the
school of its involvement in the assisted places scheme was increasing because
the government was refusing to increase the level of fees for them. As a result
the school began to take many fewer pupils on assisted places, with the aim of
reducing the intake by the end of the century to some 14% of the school roll. The
head was also concerned about academic standards. These were coming under
renewed scrutiny because of the introduction of league tables for examination

Opposite page: *Cricket at Wood Lane.*

results, although it might be doubted whether they presented a fair view of the school's results since they worked against large schools catering for a reasonably wide ability range. In fact, Colin Diggory could say to the governors that "There are very few schools as large as ours with better results surviving in the fee-paying market". He could also point to the fact that as well as the outstanding results gained at A level every year, the school could also be proud of those boys whose results, while average, were an outstanding personal achievement which secured places for them on degree courses. While the constant improvement of academic standards should be a priority on the part of the school, it was important to ensure that any change in admissions policy did not radically alter the school's ethos since that remained one of Latymer Upper's great attractions to prospective parents. The head therefore concluded that the school's future lay in becoming more selective, concentrating upon academic values, and pursuing a flexible admissions policy at the ages of 8, 9, 11 and 13. (In fact the intention is also to extend the age of admission to the age of 7 in line with the trend among prep schools generally.) Most boys, however, would continue to be admitted at the age of 11 in order to retain something of the school's grammar school ethos and to sustain a commitment to primary schools, therefore "providing access to all able boys regardless of background".

Numbers overall were to remain at around 1,100 pupils, which would sustain a wide choice of GCSEs and a large sixth form. The latter was important not only for A levels but also because it was possible that post-16 education would be reformed, and large numbers would be essential to secure the wide range of courses likely to be offered. Another break with Latymer tradition, although one already commonplace in other schools, was the suggestion that girls might be admitted to the sixth form. This was generally welcomed. While such a move would probably lead to improved academic standards and have a positive influence on the sixth form, it was made primarily because the school had the staff and facilities available to cater for a perceived demand for girls' sixth form education.

Javelin, senior athletics, 1991.

The Headmaster and sixth-formers at a Forum Meeting with Malcolm Rifkind, Secretary of State for Defence, 1991.

Greater competition in the world of private education meant that change had to come if Latymer Upper was to sustain its reputation and secure its future. The maintenance of the character of the school was bound to become more difficult. Whatever the weaknesses of the assisted places scheme, it undoubtedly accounted for the continuation of the relatively wide social mix within the school. Neither the governors nor the headmaster nor the staff wanted to see the disappearance of the Latymer tradition. The way in which the school will seek to secure that tradition will be through the expansion of scholarships and bursaries to cover at least 10% of the school population. That in itself requires significant funding, which the Foundation is wealthy enough to provide; to increase the proportion to the levels common for most of the school's history would be much more difficult to achieve.

The new chemistry laboratories were opened in October 1991 by the Nobel laureate, Professor Sir Geoffrey Wilkinson. They were named the Kenneth Burton Laboratories after a former governor and Old Latymerian whose generous bequest, made after the original decision to proceed had been taken, had funded a substantial part of the scheme.

In Colin Diggory's five year plan, it was suggested that there should be included a performing arts centre and school theatre, together with a sixth form centre and improved sixth form facilities.

It went without saying that, amidst all these changes, the school should not lose sight of the wider educational scene. In June 1992 the headmaster told the governors that "education generally was experiencing a great period of change and debate within the country. It was essential that Latymer kept abreast of these developments". The main school from 11 to 16 was reorganised to meet the demands of the national curriculum with boys being grouped in the lower

Opposite page: View of the school from across the Thames. From left: the school boat house with flats above; Latymer House, accommodating the extended prep department; and Rivercourt House, the original prep department.

Links with Europe. Above left: The first European work experience group meeting at the school, 1991, with the Mayor of Hammersmith, the Headmaster and representatives of the town of Boulogne-Billancourt. Above right: The school captain on European work experience in Berlin at Tegel airport, 1994.

school from 11 to 14 at Key Stage 3 and in the middle school from 14 to 16 at Key Stage 4. End of year examinations for all years were brought back. Every boy was expected to study three sciences to GCSE level and languages were expanded to include Spanish and to allow the possibility of three languages being studied to GCSE. The teaching week was finally extended to 40 periods a week and it is hoped that "the new curriculum would gain many advantages from an increase in teaching time and a longer school day".

The range of activities available to boys was further widened. Latymer Upper has been devoting great attention upon Europe. The longstanding exchange schemes with the Johanneum and the Lycée Jean de la Fontaine still continue with success. The school has become involved in what is known as the European

Links with the Johanneum. Right: Joint orchestra rehearsal at the Johanneum. Below: Concert programme for a joint performance, 1990.

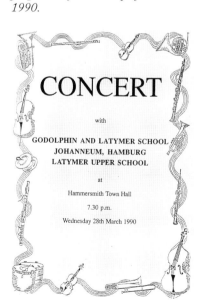

CONCERT

with

GODOLPHIN AND LATYMER SCHOOL
JOHANNEUM, HAMBURG
LATYMER UPPER SCHOOL

at

Hammersmith Town Hall

7.30 p.m.

Wednesday 28th March 1990

Dimension, which permits pupils to travel abroad for recreational purpose, and the European Work Experience scheme, which enables pupils to travel to Europe for work experience with French and German students returning to the United Kingdom for placements here immediately afterwards. The school's careers service operates an effective work placement programme for the Upper Vths in which more than a hundred and forty boys are placed every year in work ranging from the law and the media to hospitals and surgeries, the RAF and British Airways. Activities Week remains a well-established and possibly unique part of life at Latymer. The list of activities in which boys participate grows longer year by year and the following simply gives a flavour: visits to Dartmoor, North Devon, Wales, the North of England, the Highlands and Islands, Normandy, the South of France, and Scandinavia; theatre visits, gliding, sailing and windsurfing, walking, and scuba diving. Many school sports teams now have a regular opportunity to travel abroad on tour. In October 1992, for example, the senior rugby teams toured Canada while junior teams visited Ireland. There is a wide array of clubs and societies catering for all sorts of tastes. One of the most impressive is perhaps the sixth form Forum Society which has attracted many distinguished speakers in recent years, including Douglas Hurd, Michael Portillo, Malcolm Rifkind, Lord Whitelaw and Norman Tebbit.

The Latymer Upper School, like many other secondary schools, was born of the educational changes of the late nineteenth century. It has never been possible for the school to stand still. Its doors would be closed if that had been the case. But the development of the school has never been at the expense of that underlying Latymer tradition created in the first instance by C J Smith in the earliest days of the school: the provision of an academic education of the highest standard for all boys regardless of means in an atmosphere of "happy good-fellowship". In the custodianship of others, this has survived the transition to direct grant status and then its abolition. The governors remain resolute in their determination that it will also survive the more competitive situation of the late twentieth century.

Above: *Activities Week excursions.*
Below left: *Norman Tebbitt, Conservative Party chairman, addressing the Forum Society, 1991.*

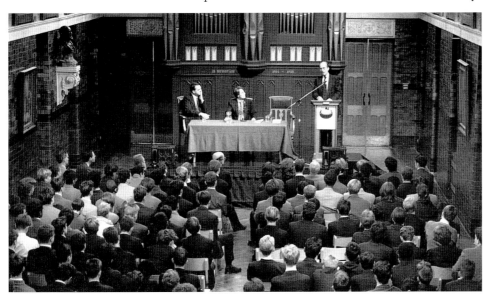

For without what the current school development plan describes as its "ethos, tolerance, good teaching, social mix and liberal approach to the understanding of all religions", the school would lose its most distinctive characteristic. Kenneth Sutcliffe was his usual perceptive self when he wrote upon his retirement in 1971 that "All headmasters know ... how much their schools owe to other people, its past and present members. These have done much to create a school's 'personality' and it is surprising how strong and how persistent a

The Headmaster with some of the 20 sixth-formers who gained places to Oxford and Cambridge in the centenary year.

school's personality can be". The fact that the school has enjoyed only seven headmasters over one hundred years has in itself been a source of continuity and stability, linking tradition on the one hand and innovation on the other.

And what of the links stretching back to the last will and testament of Edward Latymer and "Latymers poore almes boies"? The school has a long and honourable tradition in providing places for scholars from the days of the London County Council through the direct grant system to the assisted places scheme and the planned provision of Foundation scholarships and bursaries. This principle continues to this day with boys coming from a wide range of social and ethnic backgrounds. The number of local Hammersmith boys admitted to the school was a constant worry to the governors for many years but the abolition of the direct grant system and the school's subsequent independence made it impossible for Latymer Upper to maintain any semblance as a purely local school. It never had been and can never be in the future – instead its rapidly earned reputation for excellence had established a catchment area with wide boundaries from which the school still draws its pupils. Despite half-hearted efforts to remove the school from its original site, the restrictions of which have always attracted criticism yet always been overcome, Latymer Upper remains in Hammersmith, as its founder would have wished. Those local links, which the school seeks to strengthen, have always had at their core the position by right on the board of governors of the vicar and churchwarden of St Paul's, Hammersmith. The founder also asked his trustees to keep Latymer boys "from idle and vagrant courses and alsoe to instruct them in some part of God's true religion". No Latymer boy of the present day has any excuse for falling into idleness or vagrancy given the considerable range of sporting and extra-curricular opportunities available at the school. There may be some debate about what constitutes "God's true religion", but there can be no denying that today's pupils have an understanding of tolerance which stems partly from a school roll which encompasses a dozen different religions.

Today's Latymer boys enjoy an education that the founder, his original trustees and those first poor alms boys could not even have contemplated. The benefaction of a late Elizabethan gentleman nearly 400 years ago has provided an education for thousands of boys thanks to the wise administration of the Foundation by successive generations of trustees and governors. The educational aims of the Foundation have remained paramount and its independence has survived the best attempts of others to meddle with it. If the wisdom of the past is granted to others in the future, then the Latymer Foundation and with it the Latymer Upper School will continue to foster for generations to come that independent, ebullient, broad-minded and tolerant spirit which has always been the distinguishing characteristic of the Latymer boy.

Boys from the prep department, May 1995. The prep department became an independent prep school during the Centenary Year, when the Latymer Foundation founded 'The Latymer Preparatory School', formally opened by Dr J Edelman CBE, Chairman of the Latymer Foundation.

The front of the school from King Street, as it appeared in 1936.

THE HEADMASTERS OF LATYMER UPPER SCHOOL

Reverend Charles Smith MA	1895–1921
Reverend Dr Edmund Dale OBE MA D.Litt	1921–1937
Frederick Wilkinson OBE MA	1937–1957
Kenneth Sutcliffe MA	1957–1971
Maurice Isaac MA	1971–1988
Martin Pavey MA	1988–1991
Colin Diggory B.Sc C.Math FIMA FRSA	1991–

THE CHAIRMEN OF THE LATYMER FOUNDATION

E Bird	1895–1899
Reverend Prebendary J H Snowden	1899–1901
Alderman T Chamberlen JP	1901–1912
Reverend G N Walsh MA	1912–1928
Sir Marshal Hays JP	1928–1948
H H G Bennett MA	1948–1971
E W Philips MBE	1971–1988
J F G Emms	1988–1990
Dr J Edelman CBE, D.Sc, Ph.D, ARCS, C.Biol, FI.Biol	1990–

List of Distinguished Old Latymerians

The date given indicates the year of leaving Latymer Upper School

SIR JOHN JAMES WILLIAM HANDFORD (1898) *Under-Secretary of State, Scotland*

C R TANFIELD (1899) *Headmaster, Henry Compton School, London*

GEOFFREY FRANK BRADDOCK (1900) *UK Trade Commissioner*

THOMAS HAROLD HUNT CRAXTON (1901) *Professor of Pianoforte, Royal Academy of Music*

H F JAYNER (1901) *Secretary and director, Strand Hotels*

HORACE JOHN JOHNS (1901) *Under-Secretary of State, Ministry of Agriculture and Fisheries*

R C BERKINSHAW (1902) *President, Goodyear Tyre and Rubber Company*

R F JOHNSTON (A BONNET LAIRD) (1902) *Brigadier-General, broadcaster, Head of News Branch Colonial Office*

W H WADDAMS (1902) *H.M. Commissioner of Prisons*

W H HINDS (WILL HAMMER) (1903)
Founder, Hammer House Productions

ALFRED HENRY (1903) *Government Actuary*

S C P DRURY (1903) *Brigadier-General*

NORMAN F PECK (1903) *Chief Magistrate, Indian Civil Service*

P G MARR (1903) *Manager, Handley Page*

WALTER STILES FRS (1904) *Dean of Faculties of Science, University of Birmingham*

L L BURTT (1904) *County cricket player, Middlesex*

WILLIAM FREDERICK WEST (1905) *Director-General of Supplies, India Office*

T F WRIGHT (1905) *Director, Westminster Bank*

HUGH ALAN WARREN (1906) *Principal, South-East London Technical College*

R GOODMAN-CROUCH (1906) *Early pioneer of aviation*

ELY BANNISTER SOANE (1906) *Explorer and author*

J N BROWN (1906) *Assistant Comptroller, Patent Office*

G LIVENS (1907) *Professor of Mathematics, Leeds University*

E J ATKINSON (1908) *Headmaster, Newport High School for Boys*

T L WREN (1908) *Reader in Mathematics, University College, London*

SIR CYRIL EDGAR JONES KCIE (1909) *Chief Secretary to the Indian Government, Finance Department*

JOHN WARBURTON BECKETT (1909) *MP*

HARRY H.G. BENNETT (1909) *President, Chartered Institute of Secretaries; Secretary and director, J. Lyons & Company; Chairman of Governors*

SIR HAROLD SPENCER JONES FRS (1907) *Astronomer Royal*

SIR VICTOR (ALFRED CHARLES) TURNER (1910) *Secretary, Ministry of Finance, Government of Pakistan*

P C KINGSFORD (1910) *Olympic athlete*

R F C YORKE (1910) *Olympic athlete*

REGINALD LESLIE SMITH-ROSE (1912) *Director of Radio Research, Department of Science & Industrial Research*

MARTYN GREEN (1912) *Principal, D'Oyly Carte Operatic Company*

AIR COMMODORE ALAN ROBERT CHURCHMAN (1913) *Chief Inspector, Ministry of Health, Northern Ireland*

ARTHUR JAMES VICTOR GALE (1913) *Editor of* Nature

A J EDNEY (1913) *Brigadier-General*

E W HANDLEY (1914) *Assistant Secretary, Air Ministry*

W G CLEMENTS (1914) *Managing Director, Goldhawk Mutual Building Society*

REVD HERBERT DOUGLAS ANTHONY (1914) *Chief Inspector, Army Education*

GEOFFREY CHARLES VEYSEY (1914) *Under-Secretary of State, Ministry of Labour and National Service*

ALFRED JOHN NEWLING (1914) *Under-Secretary of State, Ministry of Defence*

LEOPOLD ALEXANDER PARS (1914) *President, Jesus College, Cambridge*

LOUIS H GRAY FRS (1914) *Radiation Cancer Specialist, unit of radiation named after him*

THOMAS HENRY GLASSE (1914) *Head of Foreign Office Protocol Department*

JAMES LOMAS HENDERSON (1915) *Brigadier-General*

RALPH HILL (1915) *Broadcaster, journalist*

ARTHUR J C DIXON WRIGHT (1915) *Surgeon, Vice-President, Royal College of Surgeons*

ROBERT JENKINS (1915) *MP and Mayor of Kensington*

T ALEC E LEYBURN (1915) *Director of Bowring Ltd, developed the concept of the corporate pension plan*

KINGSLEY BRICE SPEAKMAN SMELLIE (1915) *Professor of Economic History, London School of Economics*

R C J HOWLAND (1915) *Professor of Mathematics, University of Southampton*

LESLIE SLOT (1916) *Property developer*

W J FIELD (1916) *MP*

M WILLSON-DISHER (1916) Daily Mail *drama correspondent and author*

ANTHONY HOLLIS (1916) *Actor and film star*

WALTER LEGGE (1916) *Founder, the Philharmonic Orchestra*

DAVID JOHN ROWLAND EVANS (1916) *Director, Phoenix Assurance Co. Ltd*

E W WHELLER (1916) *Olympic athlete*

CHARLES EDWARD WOOD (1917) *Director, Midland Bank*

E P PETER (1918) *Olympic water polo player*

SIDNEY HARRISON (1918) *Concert pianist, author and broadcaster*

SIR RALPH LACEY (1918) *Cotton Controller, Chairman of the Royal Cotton Commission*

L A DUNTHORNE (1918) *General Manager, Cornhill Insurance*

ALFRED COBBAN (1919) *Professor of French History, University of London*

BENJAMIN FRANKEL (1919) *English composer*

R E WHITMAN (1921) *Lord-Lieutenant of Middlesex*

B A BATEMAN (1921) *England amateur soccer player*

E W WALKER (1921) *Director of Education, Bedford*

NORMAN CLARIDGE (1922) *Actor*

ARTHUR CHARLES FREDERICK BEALES (1922) *Professor of History of Education, King's College, London*

JOHN WILLIAM BELCHER (1922) *MP, Parliamentary Secretary to Board of Trade*

REVD CANON CHRISTOPHER D WADDAMS (1922) *Fellow and Senior Tutor, St Catherine's College, Cambridge*

LOUIS HAYWARD (1922) *Film star*

LEONARD V CHILTON (1923) *President, Royal Photographical Society*

REVD CANON ERIC LIONEL MASCALL (1923) *Professor of Historical Theology, King's College, London*

S C MERCER (1923) *Olympic diver*

STANLEY FRENCH (1924) *Theatre impresario*

J C HEAP (1924) *Olympic 100 metres runner*

PHILIP JOSEPH SYNETT (1925) *Professor of Botany, University of Swansea*

WILLIAM LANCELOT FRANCIS (1925) *Secretary, Science Research Council (DSIR)*

DONOVAN CHILTON (1926) *Keeper, the Science Museum, London*

BERNARD PAUL STANNEY (1926) *Headmaster, Raines Foundation School, London*

C R C M HAMMOND (1926) *President, National Union of Bank Employees*

CHARLES MCEVOY (1926) *Playwright*

RONALD WALTER DOUGLAS (1927) *Professor of Glass Technology, University of Sheffield*

GERALD RAYMOND BURT (1927) *Chief Secretary, British Railways Board*

GEORGE L SHEPPARD (1927) *Administrative and Establishment Officer, London Fire Brigade*

LESLIE T WADDAMS (1928) *Headmaster, Sir Joseph Williamson's Mathematical School, Rochester*

NATHAN GOLDENBERG (1928) *Scientific Adviser, Marks & Spencer*

HIS HONOUR JAMES WILLIAM BROOME (1928) *Chief Justice, Allahabad, India*

NICHOLAS POLUNIN (1928) *Environmental conservationist and explorer*

JOHN ELIOT HARDY MOSS (1928) *Chief Agricultural Adviser, Shell Chemical Company*

CYRIL HODGE (1928) *Overseas Manager, Guardian Assurance Group*

STUART HAVELOCK HOLLINGDATE (1929) *Director of Computing, University of Birmingham*

MAURICE STEVENSON BARTLETT FRS (1929) *Professor of Bio–Mathematics, University of Oxford*

DAVID SHOENBERG FRS (1929) *Professor of Physics, University of Cambridge*

A S E TRAYFORD (1929) *Executive Director, Association of Insurance Brokers*

ARTHUR NEWMAN (1929) *Group Director of Development, Wellcome Foundation*

JOHN VEATS (1929) *Director of Finance and Administration, Institute of Directors*

DAVID WATTS (1930) *Managing Director, George Wimpey Co. Ltd*

KENNETH J BURTON (1931) *Master of the Company of Actuaries*

ALAN JOHN PITTS CRICK (1931) *Director of Economic Intelligence, M.o.D.*

IAN FRANCIS BROOK (1931) *Executive Director, Grange Film Productions*

T HARPER SMITH (1932) *Headmaster, St Marks Secondary School, London*

A HANSON (1932) *Director and producer of "In Town Tonight"*

E A BLACKALL (1932) *Professor of German Literature, Stanford University. California*

JOHN EDWARD CURTIS PREBBLE (1932) *Writer, novelist, historian*

RICHARD L F SOUTHWOOD (1932) *Olympic Gold Medallist in double sculls*

C A F MEEKINGS (1933) *Librarian, Public Records Office, author*

R OGILVIE (1933) *Olympic pairs skater*

SIR ROBERT JAMES CLAYTON (1933) *Technical Director, General Electric Company plc*

EDWIN WILLIAM PHILLIPS (1934) *Director, Lazard Brothers, Chairman, Friends Provident Life Office, Chairman of Governors*

J R M DRYDEN (1934) *General Secretary, Society of Civil Servants*

TERENCE TILLER (1934) *Poet, pioneer radio producer*

HENRY DRYDEN (1934) *Head of GCHQ, Operations Division*

KENNETH JAMES UFFEN (1934) *Ambassador and UK Permanent Representative OECD, Paris*

JOHN STANLEY SAWYER FRS (1934) *Director of Research, Meteorological Office*

WALLACE W BRIGDEN (1934) *Consultant, London Hospital*

DOUGLAS CRAIG (EHD JONES) (1934) *Professor, Royal College of Music, Director Sadler's Wells*

CECIL FREDERICK RAWNSLEY (1935) *"Cats' Eyes" – famous wartime night fighter navigator*

RONALD PITTS CRICK (1935) *Ophthalmic surgeon*

HENRY GEORGE STEWART (1935) *Director of Studies, Britannia Royal Naval College, Dartmouth*

HAROLD TREVOR MOTE (1936) *First Mayor of the London Borough of Harrow*

G FRICKER (1936) *Chief Executive Officer, Nyasaland Government*

MAJOR-GENERAL JOHN TURNER STANYER (1936) *Director-General, Supply Co-Ordination M.o.D.*

137

WALTER FLACK (1936) *Financier, City Centre Properties*

GERALD ARTHUR CHAPMAN (1936) *Executive Board member, British Airways Authority*

JOHN BAYLISS (1937) *Author and poet*

SHAUN ALFRED GRAHAM SUTTON (1937) *Head of Drama Group BBC, TV*

JAMES LAWRENCE KING (1937) *Regius Professor of Engineering, Edinburgh University*

CYRIL W CIMA (1937) *Life Manager, Guardian Assurance Group*

MICHAEL LAWRENCE FRANCIS (1937) *Regional director, Midland Bank*

JOHN FREDERICK CHARLES SPRINGFORD (1937) *British Council Representative, Canada*

R D BIRCH (1938) *Director of Education, Berwick*

RONALD WILLIAM THOMAS BRAY (1938) *MP, Lloyd's Underwriter*

SIR JOHN KILLICK GCMG (1938) *Ambassador to USSR and NATO, Deputy Under-Secretary of State, Foreign and Commonwealth Office*

JOHN FREDERICK GEORGE EMMS (1938) *Deputy Chairman, Commercial Union; Chairman of Governors*

DENNIS WOOLEY (1938) *Senior Manager, Exchange and Control Department, Bank of England*

DENNIS H GREEN (1939) *Schröder Professor of German, University of Cambridge*

G D OAKLEY (1939) *Davis Cup player*

J E SEWELL (1939) *Parliamentary journalist,* Daily Telegraph

LAURENCE JOSEPH SAPPER (1939) *General Secretary, Association of University Teachers*

GORDON ALASTAIR HUTCHINSON (1939) *Controller and Auditor-General, United Republic of Tanzania*

SIR IAN PERCIVAL QC (1939) *MP, Solicitor-General, Recorder of Deal*

ERIC WALLER (1939) *Headmaster, Walpole Grammar School, Ealing*

LEONARD MARTIN BROAD (1939) *Assistant Secretary, Export Credits Guarantee Dept, Department of Trade and Industry*

S C WOOD (1940) *Chief Education Officer, Uganda*

D A T THAIN (1940) *International Civil Servant; General Secretariat Council of Ministers, European Community*

DONALD RAMSEY FRS (1940) *Head of the Spectroscopy Division, National Research Council of Canada*

KENNETH SYKORA (1941) *BBC interviewer and Compère*

SIR JAMES SPICER (1941) *MP, Chairman of Conservative Group for Europe*

KENNETH L MAIDMENT (1942) *President of Columbia Pictures; President of BAFTA*

DOUGLAS ARTHUR COLE (1942) *Poet, journalist,* Daily Telegraph

M H QUENOUILLE (1942) *Professor of Statistics, Yale University*

CHARLES ERNEST HOWICK (1942) *Assistant Secretary, Inland Revenue*

PHILIP JOSEPH SYNETT (1943) *Professor of Botany, University of Swansea*

PETER WILLIAM WHATTON (1943) *Deputy Vice-Chancellor, University of Melbourne*

IAN PASHLEY GIBB (1944) *Director and Keeper, British Library*

GEOFFREY STUART LUDFORD (1944) *Professor of Aeronautical Engineering, Cornell University, USA*

NOEL HENRY BEADLE (1944) *Assistant General Manager, Barclays Bank plc*

ARTHUR JAMES HENRY CHADBOND (1945) *Headmaster, Laindon Comprehensive School, Basildon*

(ALFRED) KENNETH EDWARDS (1944) *Deputy Director-General, Confederation of British Industry*

DOUGLAS GEORGE MAURICE DOSSER (1945) *Professor of Economic Theory, University of York*

BRYAN SKINNER (1945) *Founder, Crest Homes*

VICTOR W E MOORE (1945) *Professor of Law, University of Reading*

JOHN HARDY STUART (1945) *President, Institute of Chartered Secretaries and Administrators*

ALAN WATSON (1946) *Olympic oarsman*

STANLEY FREDERICK ST CLAIRE DUNCAN (1946) *Ambassador to Bolivia, High Commissioner to Malta*

DAVID WALDER (1946) *MP, novelist*

HENRY EDGAR HALL FRS (1946) *Professor of Physics, University of Manchester*

PETER COE (1946) *Theatre director*

ALISTAIR STEWART MACMILLAN (1947) *Headmaster, Glenburn High School, Skelmersdale New Town*

R M HARRISON (1947) *Olympic fencer*

ALAN LOUIS JEFFREY SAPPER (1947) *General Secretary, Association of Cinematography, Television and Allied Technicians; Chairman, TUC General Council*

JOHN BULLOCK (1947) *Joint Senior Partner and Deputy Chairman, Coopers & Lybrand*

MICHAEL EDWARD NELSON (1947) *Chairman, Reuters Foundation*

MAJOR-GENERAL DAVID HOUSTON (1947) *President, the Regular Commission Board, Lord Lieutenant of Sutherland*

WILLIAM ARTHUR BENNETT (1948) *Director of Research, Applied Linguistics, University of Cambridge*

PETER EDWARD WALKER (Lord Walker of Worcester PC) (1948) *MP, Secretary of State for Trade and Industry, Energy, Wales*

G A RENDELL (1948) *Professor of Organisational Behaviour, University of Bradford*

TIMOTHY JOHN BISCOE (1950) *Deputy Vice-Chancellor, University of Hong Kong*

MARTIN MAURICE BRANDON-BRAVO (1950) *MP*

HIS HONOUR ANTHONY THOMPSON QC (1950) *Circuit Judge*

NIGEL SPEARING (1950) *MP*

HARRY M GEDULD (1950) *Professor of Comparative Literature, Indiana University, USA*

MICHAEL WARD CLEGG (1950) *Assistant General Manager, BP Gas*

JOHN VINE (1950) *Vice-Chairman of N M Rothschild & Sons (C.I.) Limited*

PETER DAVIES (1951) *Director of Naval Architecture, Submarines*

RAMON FREDERICK GOODWIN (1951) *Managing Director, National Industrial Credit Company*

A T BURCH (1951) *Personnel Director, Sainsbury Group*

ALAN MUMFORD (1952) *Professor of Management Development, University of Buckingham*

GEOFFREY BRIDGES (1952) *Managing Director, Cargo, British Airways*

MICHAEL JOSEPH WILMHURST (1953) *Ambassador and UK Permanent Representative, International Atomic Energy Authority (IAEA)*

MICHAEL REUPKE (1954) *General Manager, Reuters*

DAVID L BLAKE (1954) *Professor of music, University of York*

JOHN TILBURY (1954) *Concert pianist*

GEORGE NUKI (1954) *Professor of Rheumatic Diseases, University of Edinburgh*

A STOCKING (1954) *Olympic oarsman*

SIMON A F DAVIES (1955) *District Judge*

MAJOR-GENERAL ANTHONY L MEIER (1955) *Director, Defence Intelligence Support, M.o.D.*

AIR VICE-MARSHALL JEFFERSON MACKEY (1955) *Director, Defence Dental Services, M.o.D.*

GRAHAM SARGEANT (1955) *Financial Editor, Sunday Times*

KENNETH MASON GWILLIAM (1955) *Professor of Transport Logistics, Erasmus University, Rotterdam*

SIR ROGER DENIS MOATE (1956) *MP*

VICTOR WEST (1956) *Chief Executive, Royal National Pension Fund for Nurses*

RICHARD NELSON PERHAM FRS (1956) *Professor of Biochemistry, University of Cambridge, President of St John's College, Cambridge*

DAVID PILBEAM (1957) *Professor of Social Science and Director of the Peabody Museum, University of Harvard*

NORMAN DANKIN (1957) *Managing Director, Schroder Finance Ltd*

BRIAN JOHN RIX (1957) *Director, Chubb Security Ltd*

FREDERICK JOHN VINE FRS (1957) *Professor, Environmental Sciences, University of East Anglia*

DAVID STILES (1957) *Professor of Chemistry, Acadia University, Canada*

BEYAN P NORTHCOTT (1957) *Music critic,* The Independent

GRAHAM ANGEL (1957) *The Receiver, Metropolitan Police*

NIGEL LEONARD WOOLNER (1957) *Architect, Senior Partner, Chapman Taylor Partners*

HUGH SEELEY (1958) *Surgeon*

GEORGE GORDON HARVEY WALDEN (1958) *MP, Parliamentary Under-Secretary of State, DES, Columnist* Daily Telegraph

ALAN JOHN COE (1958) *Assistant Secretary-General, Royal Institute of Chartered Surveyors*

JOHN H SHEPHERD (1958) *Television producer and director*

CHRISTOPHER PAUL GLASSON (1959) *President, Allsteel Inc. USA*

ROBIN FAIRHURST (1959) *Operatic singer*

MICHAEL STUART THOMAS (1959) *MP, Vice-President, Social Democratic Party*

ALAN CHARLES HUNT (1959) *Consul-General of Trade and Investment Promotion, Germany*

JOHN LAWRENCE WHITTY (1960) *General Secretary of the Labour Party*

REAR-ADMIRAL MICHAEL R THOMAS (1960) *President of the Ordnance Board, M.o.D.*

DAVID VIVIAN RICHARDSON (1960) *Chief Executive, Hallé Concerts Society, Manchester*

RICHARD CUTTING (1961) *Director, Research and Development Centre, Cambridge*

ANTHONY HOSE (1962) *Musical Director, Welsh National Opera Company*

IAN WRIGHT (1962) *Professor and Head of English, Australian National University*

ROBERT M CUSHMAN (1962) *Theatre critic,* The Observer

JOHN BURGESS GODDARD (1962) *Henry Dayish Professor of Regional Development Studies, University of Newcastle*

AIR COMMODORE BRIAN E PEGNALL (1963) *Director of Air Operations, M.o.D*

PAUL STRONG (1964) *Headmaster, William Farr Church of England Comprehensive School, Welton*

PHILIP FRANCIS DAVID HODGE (1964) *Financial Controller, Yellow Pages International*

ALAN RICKMAN (1964) *Actor and film star*

GUY CHRISTOPHER MARRIOTT (1965) *Senior Vice-President, EMI Music, USA*

REVD CANON JOHN BARTON (1966) *Professor of Theology, University of Oxford*

NIK K GOWING (1966) *Diplomatic Editor, Channel 4 News, ITN*

MICHAEL DAVID KENNETH FOOT (1966) *Deputy Director, Supervision and Surveillance, Bank of England*

MARTIN TIMBRELL (1966) *Editor,* Stock Exchange Yearbook

LESLIE GABRIEL VALIANT FRS (1967) *Gordon McKay Professor of Computing Science and Applied Mathematics, Harvard University*

E E JOHN SMITH (1967) *Consultant Heart Surgeon, St George's Hospital, London*

JOSHUA ROZENBERG (1967) *BBC Legal Correspondent*

BARRY A SOUTHCOTT (1968) *Chief Executive, CIN Management Ltd, British Coal Pensions Funds*

RICHARD S J FRACKOWIAK (1968) *Professor of Cognitive Neurology, Institute of Neurology, London*

RAFAEL S. WALLFISCH (1969) *Cellist*

PETER N H POPHAM (1969) *Journalist,* The Independent

NORMAN R BLACKWELL (1970) *Head of the Policy Unit, the Prime Minister's Office*

HILARY JONES (1970) *The TV Doctor*

DEYAN SUDJIC (1970) *Architectural correspondent, Executive Director, Blueprint*

MICHAEL P STEAN (1970) *Chess grand-master, journalist and author*

PAUL HODGES (1970) *Managing Director, ICI Watercare Division*

DAVID B JORDAN (1970) *BBC Chief political advisor*

SUMIR SHAH (1970) *BBC Head of political programmes*

HUGH R JONES (1970) *Winner, London Marathon and Olympic runner*

ANTHONY JOHN FREEDMONT (1971) *Professor of Pathology, University of Manchester*

ALMAR BATI (1971) *Journalist,* The Spectator

TREVOR A WOOLLEY (1971) *Head of Resources and Programmes (Army) M.o.D.*

TAYLOR DOWNING (1971) *Television producer*

MAX H EILENBURG (1971) *Publishing Director, Secker & Warburg and Minerva Books*

CHRISTOPHER GUARD (1971) *Actor and film star*

MEL SMITH (1971) *Actor, writer and director*

PETER G HENDY (1971) *Managing Director, Centre West Bus Company Ltd*

RICHARD HAYWARD (1972) *County cricketer, Middlesex and Hampshire*

JAMES CUTHBERT SMITH FRS (1972) *Head, Laboratory of Developmental Biology, National Institute of Medical Research*

JULIAN BORGER (1972) *BBC Foreign Correspondent*

STEPHEN HODGES (1972) *Managing Director, Close Brothers Limited*

CHARLES MORGAN (1972) *Drummer to Elton John*

DOMINIC GUARD (1974) *Actor and film star*

WILLIAM JOHN EMMOTT (1974) *Editor,* The Economist

STEPHEN THOMAS CROWNE (1974) *Chief Executive, Further Education Development Association*

PETER J YAUN (1974) *Marketing Analyst Manager, Trustee Savings Bank*

NIGEL KEITH ANTHONY STANDISH VAZ (1975) *MP*

DAVID CESARANI (1975) *Professor of Modern Jewish Studies, University of Manchester*

JOHN WRIGLESWORTH (1975) *Director of Strategy, Bradford and Bingley Building Society*

MATTHEW G S BOND (1978) *Journalist,* The Times

HUGH GRANT (1978) *Actor and film star*

SIMON D HENDERSON (1978) *Captain of Rosslyn Park RUFC*

COLIN STONE (1978) *Concert pianist*

SIMON P HUGHES (1978) *County cricketer, Middlesex and Durham, journalist and broadcaster*

ANDREW HOLMES (1978) *Olympic rowing Gold Medallist*

MATTHEW N K KNEALE (1978) *Novelist*

PHILIP GRABSKY (1979) *Television producer and director*

EDWARD A M PILKINGTON (1979) *Journalist,* The Guardian

NICHOLAS GRANGER TAYLOR (1981) *Artist*

ANDREW HALES (1982) *Composer, keyboard player, Sade*

RICHARD C PHELPS (1983) *Olympic oarsman*

MICHAEL NYMAN (1985) *World Scrabble Champion*

JUSTIN G WALTERS (1985) *Fellow of All Souls*

Index